By Force *and* Fear

By FORCE and FEAR
A Stolen Homeland

ANNA UNGER GOODWIN

By Force and Fear
A Stolen Homeland

Copyright © 2024 by Anna Unger Goodwin

All rights reserved. This book or parts thereof may not be reproduced in any form without prior written permission, except by a reviewer who may quote brief passages in a review to be printed in magazines, newspapers, or on the web.

For questions or information regarding permission for excerpts or to purchase books in bulk, please contact Bitterroot Mountain Publishing House at Editor@BMPHmedia.com

This is a work of creative nonfiction. Although the author and publisher have made every effort to ensure the validity of the stories in this book, we assume no responsibility for error, inaccuracies, omissions, or any inconsistency herein. All slights of people, places, and organizations are unintentional.

Interior and cover design by Stephanie Anderson
Photographs: All images in the author's collection
Edited by Jennifer Leo

Library of Congress Cataloguing-in-Publication Data

ISBN: 978-1-960059-27-7 (Softcover)
ISBN: 978-1-960059-26-0 (eBook)

Printed in the United States of America
10 9 8 7 6 5 4 3 2 1

Published by:

Bitterroot Mountain Publishing House LLC

PRAISE FOR
By Force and Fear

"In stunning and wonderfully described detail, we journey with Anna Goodwin through her father's stories of her families escape from war-torn Russia during the Bolshevik Revolution. Sitting on her father's knee safe in Canada, she learns of her family's traumatic flight to freedom in the West. This book is a must read for those who love to discover history and its cost through the eyes of the people who lived it."
                              Sarah Vail
                              Award Winning Author

"By Force and Fear, Anna Goodwin's story of her father's escape from Russia during the Bolshevik revolution, is poignant, riveting, and very relevant to today's world. Whether we are reminded of Ukrainians fleeing Russian aggression or of Palestinians caught in a conflict that has destroyed any sense of peace or home, Goodwin reminds us of how powerful that word "home" is, and what it means to be a refugee. As she vividly describes her father's experiences, the reader feels that they are there with her family, desperately seeking a new, safe, peaceful place to live.

    Goodwin's father became a refugee at the age of 12. She tells her father's accounts through her own memories of the stories he told her when she was a youngster in Canada. Through her memory of her father's courageous flight, she retells how dangerous his family's escape was, and how lucky we are to live in a free country. When finally safe in Canada, he would remind his family, "Children, you have no idea how lucky you are to live in a free country. Never, never let your freedoms go."

As Anna's father and family shared stories of those terrible years as refugees, her grandfather summed it up best, saying, "More than anything, what we learned in those years is that we are all God's children. And we all deserve kindness, help, and love. It doesn't matter what color, country, religion, or culture people come from." Goodwin's book reminds us of our shared humanity and of the heartbreak of being forced to flee from one's home under terrifying circumstances. Her message is one of love.

As the granddaughter of a Volga German whose family lost everything during the revolution, I was better able to understand, through Goodwin's narrative, my own grandfather's journey to the United States. Grandpa Steinmetz served in the Czar's army before immigrating to the U.S. in 1912. His mother, still in Russia, never received the money he sent to her and starved to death during the Bolshevik revolution.

Ethel Steinmetz Marmon
Granddaughter of a Volga
German-Russian

"This piece of history written by Anna Goodwin is gripping. I could not put it down. I was there in the center of the story which takes us through anguish and the depths of suffering and humanity. And still it is uplifting in the Goodness, Kindness, Love, and Courage of humanity. Stunning!"

Neil Bricco MS, LCPC
Psychotherapist in private practice,
Author of *Wisdom of the Wound*

This book is dedicated to my greatest teachers: Cornelius and Anna Unger, Grandpa and the aunties, as well as all the refugees who to this day still live in terror and are disenfranchised in their own country, as well as the world.

TO THE READER

PLEASE NOTE AS you read, these stories are written from my point of view as a child and teenager, under the title *Anna,* and also from my dad's point of view as a twelve and thirteen year old German-Russian boy, *Chnals.* Many of the stories were passed on to me in German by my father and his family. They are written as I remember them.

By Force and Fear is based on the personal and heartrending accounts, first of my family's escape from Russia to Ukraine during the Russian Revolution, and the communist takeover, and then from Ukraine, to Canada, at the beginning of the Stalin era. For six years they ran and hid in terror as anarchists pillaged their villages, and the red and black armies killed thousands of people in the German settlements.

Although they were not told to me in the sequence I have written them, I have arranged the stories in such a way that you can follow the journey as it unfolded. I have attempted to stay as true to the original narratives and writings of my father, family, and friends as possible, without sacrificing the continuity and emotional validity of their flight. The book also includes information from writings and stories of other survivors. I have extensively used the German book *The Tereker Ansiedlung* by

C.P. Toews, 1945, that my father gifted me, as well as historical accounts of that time. Some of the names of people have been changed.

Now I pass these stories on to you so you too can know what so many refugees from countless countries have experienced as they flee their homeland, often under murderous and cruel dictatorships, to struggle and find freedom and safety for themselves and their children. I will look at how the unthinkable trauma many have experienced affected them, and also their children who were born in the new and safe country, both in a negative and positive way.

OTHER BOOKS WRITTEN BY THE AUTHOR

NON-FICTION

Sandplay Therapy: A Step by Step Manual for Psychotherapists of Diverse Orientations
Barbara L. Boik and E. Anna Goodwin
Published by WW Norton, (2000)

How to Cope with Stress after Trauma:
Especially for Veterans, their Families, and Friends
E. Anna Goodwin MS, NCC
Published by Bitterroot Mountain Publishing House (2014)

A Path Beyond Post Traumatic Stress
Steps to Recovery and Resilience
E. Anna Goodwin MS, NCC
Published by Bitterroot Mountain Publishing House (2019)

FICTION

Justice Forbidden
Ana Parker Goodwin
Published by Bitterroot Mountain Publishing House (2011)

CONTENTS

To the Reader. ix
Other Books Written by the Author. xi
History of the German People in Russia. xvii
Introduction. xxi
1   The Tereker Settlement, February 1918. 1
2   The Tatars are coming 9
3   Men vote to leave or stay 21
4   Escape from the Tereker Villages 31
5   Traveling to Kasi Jurt. 45
6   Arrival in Kasi Jurt. 59
7   Kasi Jurt. 67
8   Where now?. 75
9   Left Behind 81
10   Rescue 87
11   Kostek 93
12   Photos 97
13   On the Road to Chassow Jurt 101
14   On the Train to SuworowkaThe Birth of a Sister 111

15 Arriving in Suworowka	121
16 The Widow Derksen's Farm	131
17 The Red Army Soldiers	139
18 Preparing to Leave	155
19 Bakhmut, Ukraine	167
20 Ukraine at War: The Black Army	181
21 Escape	191
Reflections	197
Letters from Russia, 1976–1993	203
Name Changes in Canada	205
Acknowledgements	207

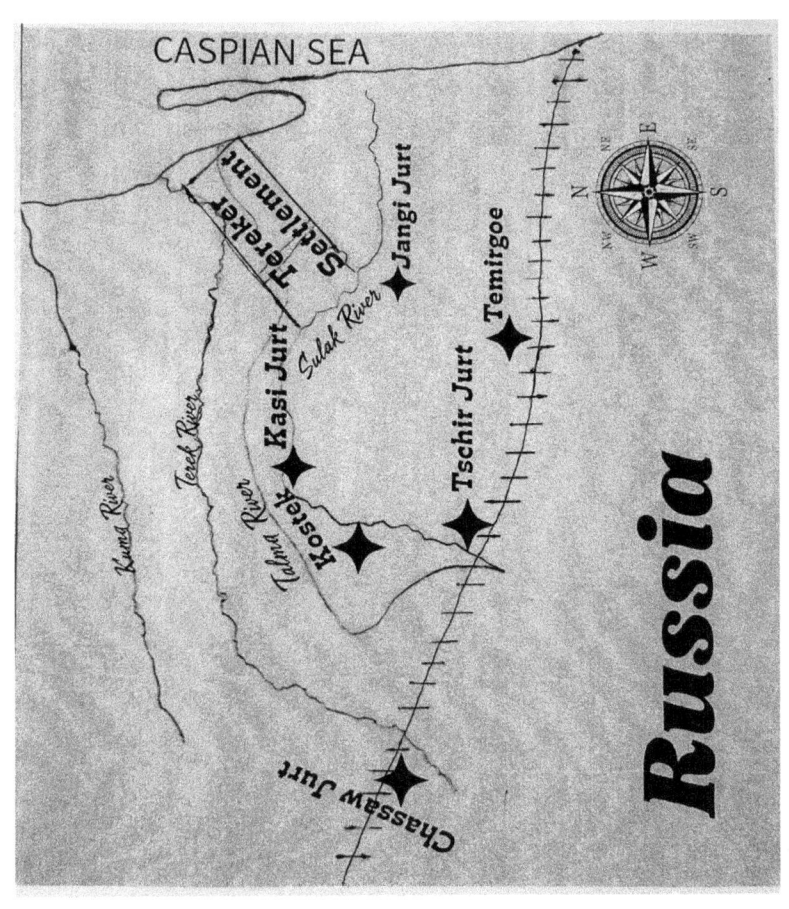

Southern Russia on the Caspian Sea north of the Caucasus Mountains. Tereker Settlement and Muslim villages nearby.

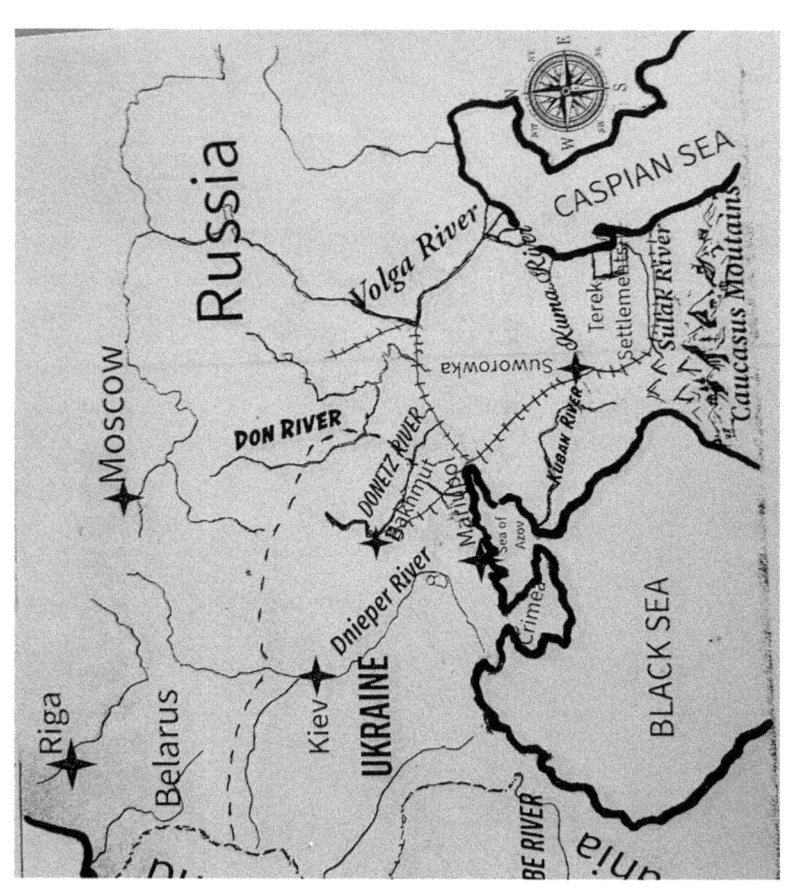

Trip from Southern Russia to Bakhmut, Ukraine

HISTORY OF THE GERMAN PEOPLE IN RUSSIA

WHEN I TELL people my dad's stories many ask, *"Why were there so many German people in Russia?* Here is a little of the history that will help you understand.

The history of German migration to Russia started with a marriage and a murder. On August 21, 1745, Catherine, a German national, married Peter III of Russia to create an alliance between Germany and Russia. On July 9, 1762, Catherine led a *coup d'état*, and had her husband arrested. He was murdered eight days later while in custody. At that time Catherine became the first Czarina of all of Russia. Her goal was to upgrade a backward country.

Early on, Catherine the Great realized that food in Russia was scarce and farming lagged far behind her homeland, Germany. The Russian people did not use any of the modern machinery or methods of farming, and thus she signed a decree (*ukaz*) to welcome farmers from many areas of Europe. However, she especially solicited farmers from Germany and Prussia, and offered special incentives for European's to immigrate to Russia. If they taught the people how to farm, she would give them land and many privileges the other Russians did not have.

INCENTIVES:

1. Land: Most were given land in fertile Ukraine: 30 hectares (75 acres) or more
2. Initial financial assistance
3. The freedom to retain their own language
4. The free and unrestricted practice of religion
5. Exemption from military service
6. Self governance and tax breaks

Within the first five years of Catherine's program, thirty-thousand people immigrated to Ukraine, around the St. Petersburg area, the Black Sea, and the Volga River. Over one hundred new villages developed. By mid 1800s a half million settlers had arrived, most of them Protestants because of the ongoing religious wars with the Catholic Church in Europe.

In Russia, many of the German people were not a poor people. As a matter of fact, many were quite rich in property, money, silver, and gold. And these riches became both their fortune and their downfall. Over time, Ukraine, farmed largely by the German people, developed into the bread basket of Russia, and many German people became very wealthy. Numerous Russians worked for them. And understandably, the ethnic people grew envious of the Germans, who had been given privileges none of them had in their own homeland.

As the German villages grew, the Germans bought large tracts of land elsewhere in Russia to settle and rehabilitate. My grandparents left Ukraine in 1903 and settled in the Caspian Sea area, just north of the Caucasus Mountains in Dagestan, fairly close to Iran. The German settlers built a wooden dam and twenty miles of canals so they could irrigate the salt pepper filled loom to make it usable. They grew fruit, sugar cane, and vegetables as well as wheat. They milled the wheat, selling the flour and fruit to that southern region. The settlement expanded to seventeen villages although only fifteen were actually populated before the Russian Revolution.

Although the incentives had been revoked in the late 1800s, Czar Nicolas II, who came to the throne in 1896, mostly still honored the agreement with the German people. He was dethroned in 1917 when the Russian Revolution began, and was later killed. When Lenin and the Red Communists took over, Lenin removed Russia from WWI, and the German people living in Russia were persecuted. They lost their right to democratic self-governance, all their land, freedom of speech and religion. Furthermore, they were forced into military service.

During the revolution and the early Stalin purges, many of the people were killed. Others fled to the USA and Canada as refugees, or were sent to labor camps in Siberia to work in the mines. One-third did not survive. After the Soviet Union collapsed in 1989, many of the German people in Russia migrated to Germany. Some remain in Russia to this day. In late 1976, my father found and contacted his cousin in Bakhmut, and began to correspond with her. I still have those letters (See Letters from Russia).

When I was a child, my father would often listen to the radio reports about the Korean War. He would look deeply into my eyes, and with his voice shaking would say, "Anna, never let your freedoms go….never let your freedoms go."

INTRODUCTION

AS I SIT in my favorite chair watching television, I am stunned to see thousands of refugees stream into Europe from Ukraine as Russian bombs blow up their world. Why? Why is this happening again? I feel sudden tears sting my eyes. I can only imagine the agony these people and their children are enduring. But mine are also special tears–tears for my ancestors–my father and his family who escaped Ukraine in 1924 after the Russian Revolution, and the beginning of the Stalin era.

I think of how soon we have forgotten that we are all immigrants, all one people. How these are the people who have made the Americas great. We have forgotten—, or we never knew—, the courage it took, and the struggles our families and others from all lands went through to come to countries more free than their homeland.

As a child, and through my teens, my mother, father, sister and I lived on an ordinary farm on the plains of Manitoba, on miles and miles of flat prairie lands. But somehow, I always considered my family to be special. Why? Not only had my father and his family survived the Russian Revolution and the great, Russian famine of 1921-1922, and then escaped Communism to come to Canada, but we had an extra Thanksgiving Day. One at the beginning of October, like all other Canadians, and one on August 8th, the day my father's family arrived on free soil.

In August my aunties, my dad, my uncle, and grandfather told stories of what they remembered. Instead of turkey we ate *varenike* (cottage cheese in flour pockets, boiled, and served with butter gravy) the favorite meal of the family during their escape to freedom.

My father wasted no words. Nor did he smile or laugh a lot. He was a stern German- Russian, immigrant farmer—a strong man, not in stature, but in mind and spirit. Life was serious business to him. But every so often I could convince him to tell me stories—stories of how he and his family—his parents, seven sisters and one brother—fled Ukraine via Riga, Latvia, in the hull of a British ship. As a result, my father, as well as his brother and two oldest sisters, suffered from Post Traumatic Stress most of their lives.

Dad was one of the greatest perfectionists I have ever met. And in what did my sister and I have to be perfect? In everything. He was afraid that if we made any mistakes, something terrible might happen. What Dad valued most for our future was education. Even as a youngster, he pressured me to do my very best in school. Nothing else was acceptable. And he was very proud of me because I always got A's on my report card. Whenever I read or did my homework, neither of my parents interrupted me—not even to do the dishes or feed the chickens. And wow, did I take advantage of that!

"Anchen," my father would say, "You have no idea how lucky you are to be able to go to school and study. This is your job. Do it right."

I remember when he joined the school board so he could vote out our present teacher, not because the man was a bad person, but because he was an ineffectual teacher. Dad decided he hadn't taught the kids in our small country school what we needed to learn, to be able to go on to high school and beyond. It wasn't until later that I understood the reason for his obsession with education.

Dad, thank you for that gift.

STORY 1
The Tereker Settlement, February 1918

ANNA

IN THE EVENING *after all the chores were done, still in his overalls and long-sleeved checkered cotton shirt, my dad would sit in the living room on our brown leather sofa and read* Der Bote, *a German weekly paper. And I would quietly climb up beside him before I went to bed, tucking my frilly and flowered cotton skirt over my knees. I still remember the smell of homemade chicken soup and fried potatoes that lingered in the air from supper.*

"Anchen," Dad would say in German, the only language we were allowed as children to speak at home—just in case we'd confuse the German and English languages. "Young children like you should be in bed by now."

"But Dad, I'm nine years old. And look." I pointed out the window. *"Even the sun hasn't gone to bed."*

"No excuses," he would mutter. "You know the sun doesn't go down here in Manitoba until after 9pm in summer." He turned to my mother, who sat in the oak rocking chair nearby embroidering a picture of a peacock I now have hanging in my bedroom. Her

long dark hair tumbled down on her shoulders as she bent over the picture. "Mother," Dad said. "Put her to bed."

My fourteen-year-old sister, Lee, who sat at the dining room table doing her homework, glanced up and frowned. I knew she was mad at me for making a fuss, but I didn't care. She was bossy and I didn't like it!

I slid a little closer to him and looked into his big hazel eyes. "Just one story? A story of how you escaped from the Soviet Union when you were young?"

My father turned to me, harrumphed, and grunted. "You mean Russia. There is no Soviet Union. The Communists stole those countries!"

I checked the scowl on his face and knew I had him hooked! Smiling, I pulled my legs up onto the sofa and settled in for my story.

Dad folded the paper neatly and hung it over the arm of the sofa. Reading materials were scarce and treasured on a farm in central Canada, so far from town. The mailman came only once a week. That was if we were lucky.

"I was only twelve years old at the time," he began. "You know my name is Cornelius, but everyone calls me Chnals for short. It was during World War I, and Germany had invaded Russia." He paused. "And our family was originally from Germany, although that was very long ago." He paused again.

"Uh hu. Go on Dad," I said. I didn't understand his point. I wanted him to get to the exciting part of the story.

"Well, the Russian's were very angry with the Germans because of the war. And on top of that, the Russian people didn't have any of the freedoms the German people had in Russia, their own country."

"Why not?" I said. How strange. That wasn't fair!

His eyes drifted toward my mother, who glanced at her watch and shook her head. "That's a long story. I'll tell you later when we have more time. Anyway, the Russian people captured Czar

Nicolas II and his family, and sent them away. Everything went topsy-turvey, and no one was in charge."

"Really? Where did you live in Russia?" From the maps we had studied at school, I knew Russia was a giant country.

"Well, we lived near the Caspian Sea, on the north plains of the Caucasus Mountains. I'll show you on the map when we have a little more time. Anyway, all the soldiers and police disappeared. It's called anarchy."

I nodded my head. I thought I had heard the word in history class.

"Even the children my age knew that many young men from the mountains were coming down and robbing the German villages. The men were angry, and they killed many people. Of course, things were very different then. Even though I was only twelve, I was the oldest boy in the family. In those days, the oldest boys were always told they would need to be in charge if anything happened to the man of the house—well you know,—."

I tightened my body and moved closer to him. I knew what Dad meant. Mom glanced at him again, but said nothing."Who were these men?"I asked.

"They were called the Tatars. They were from the villages in the Caucasus Mountains and they had no money or land. They were wild! Someday you'll learn about Genghis Khan, who took over a lot of Asia and that part of southern Russia many, many, years ago. But now it's not important. Just that they were very poor and angry. They wanted what we had, even if they had to kill us all. And there were no police to stop them."

I cringed into the side of my dad's body and hung onto his overalls. "Weren't you scared?"

His eyes clouded over. He took a deep breath. At last he said, "Yes... We were very scared." Mom glanced at him again, shaking her head. Obviously she didn't want me to know the gruesome details. She always tried to protect my sister and me, even when we didn't want her to. Finally Dad swallowed hard and straightened his back. "But I had to be strong. I had to be the man, even though I was only twelve. Somehow I knew, this night they were coming for us."

I could feel my eyes turn large. I gripped my father's arm. "What happened?"

CHNALS

Feb. 6, 1918. Village #4, Konstantinowka, Southern Russia, on the Terek, a complex delta near the Caspian Sea in Dagestan, located north of the Caucasus Mountains.

Bang! Bang!

Chnals bolted upright in bed, his heart pounding hard against his wool pajamas. He gasped and jerked his head toward the dark, lace-curtained window. What was that?

Then quiet. Only blackness and the sound of the rain drumming on the shingled roof of the wood and clay house. A slight musty odor penetrated the air.

A wolf howled in the distance.

He inhaled a deep breath, blew it out slowly, and sank back against his goose-feather pillow. The noise had probably just been a board falling down on the wooden porch in the storm.

He yawned and turned over to his side, nestling back under the dark, thick, wool blanket his grandmother had made for him and his brother Gerhard to share. He'd better get some sleep. Tomorrow would be another long day of school and farm chores.

Suddenly he heard horses whinny and stomp their feet on

the hard, wet clay path outside. Then men's voices. He bolted upright in bed, and his heart began to race again. Another loud bang. This time someone pounded at the front door.

The Tatars! They were here. His mind flashed to yesterday. On the dash to school, he and Gerhard ran into some village men gathered by the muddy road. He gasped when he saw what they were staring at—two men from the villages dumped in the grassy ditch. Dead. Vultures picked at their bodies.

A few weeks earlier, these two men had gone to the Caucasus Mountains to negotiate with the Tatars imploring them to leave their German villages in peace. And now here they were. Putrid. Rotting.

For two months the settlement had been on alert, making preparations, waiting for the Tatars to descend on them. Everyone knew about the shoot-out at the mill. Several villages had already been plundered and robbed, innocent people killed by young men from the mountains. The villagers hoped and prayed this day would never come. But they knew it would only be a matter of time before they, too, would be attacked.

Chnals sucked in his breath and swallowed hard. Had their turn finally come? What should he do? Had Papa heard the pounding? No. Not likely. His and Gerhard's single plank bedroom wall adjoined the living room, but Papa and Mama's room sat at the other end of the one story house. He glanced at Gerhard beside him snuggled under the thick blanket. Chnals bent over him and checked his breathing to see if he was asleep. Gerhard inhaled, gave a little snort, and turned toward the wall. Thank heaven his little brother knew nothing. Gerhard was only nine and had always been an anxious boy.

What now? Should he run and wake up Papa? Then he remembered. Papa had left the house earlier that evening. Had he ever come back? If not—. He straightened his shoulders and took a deep breath. With Papa gone, it was all up to him. He reached under the mattress and clutched the sharp butcher knife he'd hidden on the metal frame. He whipped it out in front of him, like the pictures of men charging with swords on horseback. He had to be strong or they would all be dead by morning.

Slowly he twisted his body and slid off the homemade feather mattress. The floorboards creaked as his bare feet thumped onto the floor. Oh no! Had he wakened Gerhard? He checked his brother again. Sound asleep. He tightened his fist around the knife. Without making a sound, he tiptoed to the lace-curtained window across from the feather bed. Tugging the curtain back he stared into the darkness. Nothing. Where were the men? He was sure he had heard them. Had it all been a dream?

His mind flashed back to yesterday and the two dead men again. His brother Gerhard had run behind a bush, and Chnals heard him wretch. He could still see his father's scrunched face and hear him yell at them, "Get out of here boys. Now! *Schtikatz*!"

NO. This was NOT a dream.

Another loud knock. Then he heard Papa's firm footsteps hurry down the hall. Thank heaven Papa was home, after all. The front door squeaked open. Chnals held his breath. What if they shot his father? What would he do then?

A familiar male voice said, "We're waiting for Rudolph. He's the sentinel tonight." It was only a few of the neighborhood men. Chnals exhaled with relief and began to shake as his feet gave way, and his body almost crumpled to the floor. He hurried back to the bed and shoved the knife under the mattress.

A din of voices erupted over each other amid the thump of boots dropping on the floorboards. Then, moments later, the scraping of chairs. Chnals slid onto the bed and strained to listen.

"*Shh*. You'll wake the children," Papa said. "They're too young to know." The men's voices quieted to a murmur.

Quick! He had to know what they were saying. Without making a sound, he slid off the feather mattress again and tiptoed to the single plank wall that separated his bedroom from the main room. His fingers trembled as he pulled out the secret knot in one of the boards, nearly dropping it, then tucked it into his fist and peered through the small hole. Papa had better not find out about his eavesdropping post or there would be a "word-whipping" in store.

Seated around the homemade wooden dinner table, about fifteen feet from Chnals, four men in dripping heavy wool jackets, plus his father, fully dressed, huddled together examining a sheet of paper. Their caps lay on the table in front of them. The flame from the kerosene lamp flickered upward for a moment, and Chnals glimpsed the men's faces, their lips taut and jaws clenched.

The men whispered to each other. Chnals pressed his ear to the hole, hardly breathing. He strained to listen, but all he heard were snatches of sentences. "Russia in chaos. Order gone…" He knew that. "Czar Nicholas II and his family are prisoners of the Red Communist party. All the government soldiers have gone to join the army. There is no one left to protect us. We are on our own." He felt his jaw drop. *Oh, no!*

Chnals jerked as he heard another knock on the front door. He peered through the knothole again. His father hurried to answer. A man from Village #6 rushed in and strode to the table, his muddy boots squishing on the floor.

"Rudolph. What's happened?" Papa obviously had forgotten to keep his voice down. He closed the door and hurried after Rudolph. "We've been waiting. What did you find out?"

Rudolph pulled off his calfskin mittens and black wool cap, and tossed them on the table. His breath came fast. "They say a thousand Tatars or more with guns, on horseback, are riding down the mountains in our direction."

Chnals tightened his jaw, trying not to gasp out loud. They would all die.

"What?" The men jumped to their feet. "Are you sure?"

Papa sat up straight and stared at Rudolph. "Who told you? There are lots of rumors, you know."

Rudolph shook his head. "I talked to the man from the Muslim village next to us, whom we pay good rubles to spy for us. He speaks the truth."

Without another word from Rudolph, the men grabbed their caps, and charged to the front door. They yanked on their muddy boots, threw open the door, and rushed out. Papa tugged his cap and jacket from a hook on the wall near the door and dashed after them, letting the door slam behind him. In a few minutes all the men, including Papa and Rudolph, were gone.

Frozen, Chnals kept staring through the knothole. Horses hooves. Then all he heard was the rain drum on the roof. What should he do? Wake up Mama and the rest of the family, and hide? No, Papa would soon be back.

Finally Chnals tiptoed back to his bed.

He knelt down in prayer, fingers gripped tight. Closing his eyes, he bowed his head and whispered, "Please, please, God, keep us safe. Help me be strong."

STORY 2
The Tatars are coming

ANNA

SOMETIMES MY FATHER *took me with him while he worked on the farm, probably to give my poor mother a rest. I remember Dad hoisting me up onto the running board of the giant John Deere tractor. Then he jumped up and settled onto the black leather seat beside me. I stood next to him in my new blue jeans and purple, (my favorite color) T-shirt, holding onto the taller-than-me-fender of our tractor as he plowed the fields after harvest. I could smell the diesel fumes as they spouted into the air.*

I leaned over to Dad so he could hear me over the noise of the tractor. "Dad, please tell me another story about Russia. What happened after you heard Opa and the men say those dangerous Tatars were coming?"

He tousled my short, straight, brown hair and said, "I'm working now. Maybe another time."

"Pleeease?" *I begged.* "You said there were horrible men coming down the mountains. Who were the Tatars? Did they hurt you and Uncle Gerhard or the aunties?"

My dad frowned and stared out over the acres and acres of stubbled fields we were plowing, his jaw clenched. His voice turned gruff. "Not now," he said.

Oh, oh, I had better not make my dad angry! "Okay." *I said quietly. I never argued with my dad, but I'm sure he heard the disappointment in my voice. I stood very still, holding my head up high, as though I didn't care, and watched the yellow metal and rubber wheels go around and around, tears filling my eyes.*

We plowed in silence for a while, except for the chug, chug *of the giant green John Deere tractor. I watched as the blades of the plow turned over the wheat stubble into long, deep rows of fresh black soil. The dust tickled my nose.*

At last Dad turned to me and said, "You're right. You're old enough to know. I'll make it simple and you'll learn more, later, in school, when you study the history of Russia and the Middle East."

I remained silent.

A minute later he finally said, "You know we are Christians. We believe in Jesus as being God's son and we follow his teachings."

I nodded my head. I had heard about Jesus in Sunday school, and we used to sing: Jesus loves me this I know. I found myself singing the rest of the song in my head. For the Bible tells me so. Little ones to him belong. We are weak but he is strong.

There it was again—the word STRONG. A word my dad used a lot. You need to be strong. You need to be strong.

"Well," Dad continued. "Most of the people living near our villages were not Christians. They were Muslims."

Puzzled, I turned to him. "What are Muslims?" I had never heard the word before.

"Muslims are people who believe in, and follow the teachings of Muhammad."

"Muhammad? Who was Muhammad?"

His voice turned harsh again. "Shhhh. *Do you want me to continue or not?*"

I bowed my head and looked down, vowing to be silent.

"*There were three different kinds of Muslims who lived just south of our German villages. Like we have different kinds of Christian churches, you know.*"

Okay. That made sense. I nodded.

"*The people that were coming down from the mountains to rob us were the Tatars, and they were very poor. Like I said before, the young men were wild. Then there were two different groups just south of us.*"

I gasped, "*Were they all dangerous?*"

For the first time, my father smiled. "*No, no. The Muslims are just like any other people. There are some bad ones, but most of them are good. Do you know, Anchen? I wouldn't be alive today if it wasn't for them. They saved our lives.*"

I gasped. "*Really? They saved you?*"

"*Yes, but I'll tell you that story later.*"

I knew better than to keep asking questions. I leaned back against the fender and stayed very still. Not a peep out of my mouth. But I'd make sure to remind my father to tell me that story later.

CHNALS

February 7, 1918.
Village #4, Konstantinowka, Tereker Settlement,
Schoolhouse

The patter of rain on the roof of the two-room wooden schoolhouse roof grew louder as the morning wore on. Chnals squirmed in his chair, tapped his foot, and twisted his pencil back and forth, his mind far away.

He had slept very little all night. Early this morning, before the first cock crowed, he had heard the front door creak open, boots drop, and Papa's footsteps cross the floor. Moments later, Mama and Papa whispered to each other, but he couldn't hear what they said. Then silence.

At breakfast Papa and Mama gave stiff smiles and said, "*Guten morgen, Kinder*," as they did each morning. They mentioned nothing about a problem with the Mountain Tatars. After a breakfast of eggs and fried potatoes, Chnals, his brother, and three sisters trudged off to school on the well worn clay path through the tall grass, as usual.

"Hey buddy, are you okay?" a distant yet familiar male voice whispered.

Chnals heard the scrape of a chair as though it came from another land. In an instant he jerked his mind back to school. As he turned to look at Johann, sitting at the desk next to him, he whispered back. "Yeah, why?" He gave a quick nod and a faked smile.

Johann was his best friend. Rarely did they keep secrets from each other. But today was different. Chnals could tell no one what he thought he'd heard. What had really happened last night? Had the sentinel made a mistake? Maybe Chnals had heard wrong. Or maybe what he thought he remembered had just been a bad dream.

But what if the bandits were really coming? Were Mama and Papa safe? And what could they do to survive? The image of the dead men by the side of the road flashed over and over in his mind.

World history, then Russian language class, finally came to an end. Mr. Brandt dinged the little metal bell on his big wooden desk, signaling the beginning of the lunch recess. Arms trembling, Chnals pushed his hand-built chair back from his desk, grabbed his cap, and rushed toward the door.

"Chnals, what's the hurry?" Johann called after him.

Chnals turned and called back, "Just need a walk. I'll be right back." He stumbled out of the double doors at the back of the room, onto the porch. He had to find out *now* whether what he'd heard last night was true. Were the Tatars coming?

Shielding his eyes from the rain with his raised hands, he stared out toward the Caucasus Mountains in the south. Had something moved? A shiver ran through him.

A few minutes later he heard a horse whinny nearby. He jumped. Seconds later, a young man in heavy wool pants and a dark jacket, galloped up to the schoolhouse and dismounted. With eyes lowered, he swept past Chnals without a word and dashed into the school. A few minutes later he ran out, mounted his horse, and raced away.

The bell clanked inside, louder than usual, more urgent. Chnals felt the goose bumps on his arms rise. Something had happened. Lunch hour had barely begun. He had not yet heard his classmates open their tin lunch pails, or smelled the familiar odor of fresh bread and fish.

Chnals hurried inside to his chair, his whole body on alert. Most of the other children were already in their seats. Mr. Brandt paced back and forth in front of his desk, his hands clutched behind his tall, lean frame, his brow furrowed.

One of the children dawdled in the hallway and Mr. Brandt snapped at him. "Get in here. Now!"

Chnals drew in a sharp breath. His heart began to pound. Mr. Brandt had never raised his voice at any of the students before. And that's when he knew. The Tatars! They were coming.

Mr. Brandt stopped at the front of the classroom, released his hands, clasped them together again, and bowed his head. The class hushed. Now calm, Mr. Brandt cleared his throat and said in a strained voice, "I have some news. The Tatars are coming down the mountains." The children began to exclaim and murmur to each other in terror.

Chnals gulped and he bowed his head. His mind suddenly shifted from a harsh scream to silence. And all was quiet, except for the few words from Mr. Brandt's mouth that chirped once, then again, like deafening crickets in the night air. All he remembered later were Mr. Brandt's last words. "Go home *now*. We are in danger. The Tatars are coming, and they'll be here by morning. We must prepare to leave. If you have little brothers or sisters in Classroom One, get them now and take them home."

Chnals gulped down his fear as he remembered his father cornering him in the barn to deliver his "man-to-man" talk. That had been two months ago. Chnals had thought it strange at the time, but no one ever questioned Papa. In a stern voice he'd commanded Chnals to take charge in case of an emergency. After all, he was the oldest boy in the family and that's what oldest sons did. They took charge when their Papa left or died. Died? No, no! He had to be strong. He had to make Papa proud of him.

He straightened his back and squared his shoulders. Grabbing his metal lunch pail in one hand, he hurried over to his oldest sister, Helena, and gripped her hand in his other one, then tugged her through the crowded hallway to the next classroom. He gathered his two younger sisters and his brother, helped them on with their jackets, and marched them out the door in a line.

In less than a minute, Chnals had become a man.

On their way home, six-year-old Justina stomped her feet and whined until Chnals warned her he would tell Papa if she didn't behave. Head bent, she stumbled behind the others into the rain.

The five struggled through the long winter grass, onto the muddy path the students had engraved into the flat meadow. The sandy loam stuck to their shoes and formed a big, squashed dirt ball around them. Behind them, young children squealed with delight as they ran through the puddles, probably only knowing they were free from school. They had no idea of what awaited them. They were the lucky ones, Chnals thought.

Johann caught up with Chnals, but neither of them slapped each other on the back or tried to trip each other, as they usually did. His face white, Johann glanced at Chnals, muttered a greeting, and passed.

As they walked, Chnals gazed around him over the Tereker Settlement. This was the only home he knew. The German people had bought about 67,000 acres of land in 1901 from a wealthy feudal lord. The Tereker Settlement was a collection of 17 small German villages, but only 15 villages had been settled by this time. Now where would the people go? If they stayed, would they fight? Would they all die, like the villagers to the south? And why did the Tatars want to hurt them? Yes, the young men had always been wild, but they had never killed the German people before this last year.

Chnals jerked to alert at the sound of Gerhard's yell and Justina's scream. He wheeled around. Justina's black leather shoe was stuck in the mud, her wet flowered skirt stuck to her legs. Gerhard tried to yank her loose from the mud, but instead the shoe came off, and her foot waved in mid air. Ten-year-old Sara shook her finger at Jus and scolded her. Jus wailed. Fifteen-year-old Helena traipsed behind them, water trickling down her face and dripping off her light-brown braids. She seemed unaware.

Chnals sighed and hurried to the group. This business of being an adult had a lot fewer advantages than he had thought in the past, when he had wanted so desperately to be one of them. He grabbed Jus, flung her over his shoulder and marched toward the village. Gerhard pried the shoe loose and carried it as far away from his body as he could. For the first time, she was quiet. As if the rain had noticed the silence, it stopped as well.

As they turned onto Main Street and headed past the village windmill toward home, Chnals jerked his head toward the mill. Something was wrong. Several horse-drawn wagons splashed by on the dirt road and stopped at the front of the mill, the line growing longer each minute. The drivers rushed inside, then hurried out a few minutes later and loaded flour sacks onto their wagons. The horses galloped away as the windmill spun wildly and squeaked overhead.

Chnals stared at the wagons. It was obvious the villagers were preparing to flee. He took a deep breath and sighed with relief. Maybe they would survive. Maybe they could hide for a while and come back home after the Tatars left. And everything would be back to normal. He could swim in the Caspian Sea with his friends. Gallop his horse across the fields of tall grass. Pick ripe apricots at his grandparents' house. Even digging canals, feeding the cattle and chickens, and going to school sounded great to him now.

Cold, filthy water splattered him as the wagons rushed by, and he remembered Jus was riding on his back. She began to whine again. Chnals plunked her down on a stump near the road, grabbed a stick from the ground, and yanked her dirty leather shoe out of Gerhard's hand. He scraped off most of the mud with the stick, then shoved the shoe onto Jus's foot. "You follow me," he ordered in a stern voice he usually reserved for the horses.

The five trudged down the road again toward home. A cloud of mosquitoes buzzed around them. The girls swatted them off, but they kept coming.

Outside the blacksmith shop stood another long line of horses. The older boys and some of the men gathered to talk as they waited for the horses to be shod. Some paced back and forth with rifles slung over their shoulders. Chnals stopped for a moment, tempted to slip into the group to listen, but instead he plodded toward home. Papa had given him strict instructions to care for the family. He would prove he could be trusted.

Close to home, six men on horseback opened the gates to the community pasture and herded at least a hundred cattle and nearly as many horses onto the street. Chnals stopped and stared at them. What were the men doing? Then as though on command, he heard a familiar whinny behind him. Papa yelled, "Whoa." He turned just in time to see Papa stop the four-wheeled wagon beside them. He reached down and pulled the youngest children inside. Chnals and Helena climbed onto the back, then leaned against the edge behind the front seat where Papa sat. The other children crawled onto the sacks of flour covered with a blanket. Papa slapped the reins on the horses' hindquarters, and they raced toward home. Several geese honked overhead.

More horses and cows crossed the road. Papa glanced at the younger children, then whispered to Chnals and Helena, "The men are driving the horses and cows to a special pasture where the Tatars won't find them. When the Tatars are gone, we'll bring them home again." Chnals nodded. Helena stared out onto the distant fields of winter wheat as though she didn't hear.

Papa stopped the wagon at the front door of the house, and the children jumped down and raced inside. Chnals helped Papa unhitch the wagon and lead the horses into the wooden barn. Hands trembling, Papa removed the harnesses from the backs of the horses and hung them on hooks.

Chnals checked around to make sure all the other children were gone. Then he bent toward Papa and whispered, "When are we going to leave?"

Papa said nothing for a moment, his jaw tightening. Then he cleared his throat and said, "The village men will be meeting at the church this afternoon to vote about whether we'll leave, or stay and fight. Don't say anything to the others. Now go inside."

Chnals blinked and swallowed hard. Stay and fight? They would all die. Then he straightened his back and held his head high. He was a man now, and he would fight if he had to, but God, please, no. He turned away from Papa and strode into the house.

His four-year-old sister, Katchen, ran toward him. She was dressed in her Sunday best, a little dress trimmed with crocheted lace, long knitted white stockings, and high black leather lace-up shoes. Sweat dripped down Mama's cheeks as she fired up the wood-stove and slid in four loaves of bread. Her brow was creased, and she sang a hymn in German as she worked.

The smell of fresh bread usually made Chnals hungry, but not this time. Helena cut several slices and buttered them, pulled out some apricot jam and some cream for dipping, and placed them on the long wooden table.

A chill ran through Chnals as he sat down next to his siblings. Three sacks of salt pork were stacked at one end of the table.

Dozens of eggs wrapped in towels had been placed into a large wooden box on a nearby bench. On the floor stood two milk cans and another box filled with cabbage and carrots. How long would it take until the food was gone? They could drink river water, make bread for a while, but what then? Maybe it was better to stay and fight.

Mama dried her hands on her apron, then brought out a tin of fruit-filled cookies and some milk. She attempted a smile as she sat down next to the children. They said grace out loud in unison, as they did before each meal. *"Vater segne diese Speise, uns zum kraft und dier zum preise. Amen."* (Father, bless this meal, to our strength and to your praise.)

After they had eaten, they cleared the table as usual, and Sara washed the dishes. Mama took nine sets of tin dishes and metal cutlery out of the wood cupboard and slipped them into a clean flour sack. Then she added a few pots and pans. She never mentioned their leaving, just asked each one of the children to dress in a clean set of clothes, choose one extra set, and as long as they weren't too large, select three items they wished to take with them.

Chnals froze in his chair as reality hit. His mind went blank. Three things. That was it. How could he choose? When the other children left the table, he trudged to his bedroom. Gerhard sat in the middle of the floor, his hands covering his face. He rocked back and forth. Chnals touched his shoulder, but Gerhard pulled away. He scrambled to his feet and left the room with nothing. Chnals sighed. Gerhard had always been too quiet. Mama worried about him.

Chnals slumped down on his bed and looked around his room. A picture of the village windmill his grandmother had painted especially for him. A small wooden wagon carved by his grandfather. A bow and arrow he and Papa had made together. A blanket knitted by Mama.

He pushed back tears. At last he walked over to his chest of drawers and pulled out his nib pen, ink, and a notebook. He dressed in black wool trousers, a matching wool jacket, and a clean white shirt, then selected his newest, most practical set of extra clothes, placing his favorite cap on the pile.

He was ready to leave.

But what if the men decided to stay and fight?

STORY 3
Men vote to leave or stay

ANNA

ISN'T IT STRANGE *how there are some days we never forget? For me, that's the day I learned about the vote at the church Dad had talked about in the previous story. But not for the reason you might think.*

It was autumn and the maple trees in our five-acre yard had turned red and yellow. The day was drawing to a close. Darkness settled in around me. In the distance I heard the gray wolves howl as I did most evenings, and I howled along with them. What fun! I wished I could run with the wolves. So free, so uninhibited! After all, I was only nine years old.

As I imitated them, I darted through acres of flat land in the dusk, my growing brown hair flinging behind me. I called for my dog. "Shep! She—e-p." Usually he would bound to my side, and I'd pretend to fly, my arms outstretched, waiting for the wind to lift me.

No Shep. I stopped, glanced around me, and called again. "Shep!" Still no Shep. Where was he?

I hadn't seen him come into the barn before my father turned out the light. My very, most loved German Shepherd pooch! He was my playmate, my closest friend on our three hundred twenty acre-farm. I trained him with pieces of ginger molasses cookies I snuck out of the cookie jar. My mother guessed, but never said a word. He jumped at my command, rolled over, and shook hands. A small feat, I thought, for a dog my father had trained to go herd our twenty cows and bring them home twice a day.

I dashed back to the barn to check on him. No Shep. Just at that minute Dad turned on the yard light, then rushed outside and disappeared behind our two-story white farm house into the darkness. I heard him whistle for Shep, then again, and a minute later again. I ran into the house shouting for my mother. "Mom! Mom! Where is Shep?"

My mother hurried toward me and gave me a hug. "Anchen,, don't worry," she said. "Shep has done this before. He'll be back in the morning."

As I walked into the living room, I saw my older sister, Lee, in her jeans and blue shirt, pacing back and forth, checking the windows. Tight-lipped, she whispered, "Go to bed now. Tomorrow is Saturday. No school. Everything is fine."

I slept very little that night. In the morning I rushed outside onto the porch in my striped flannel pajamas. "Shep! Shep!" I called. I expected him to leap out from the barn to greet me like he did each morning.

Nothing.

"Shep! Where are you?" I yelled. I ran toward the giant red barn.

My father, face somber and drawn, stepped out from behind the barn carrying a dirt-covered shovel. He stiffened when he saw me and hurried toward the house. My sister peered out the barn door for a moment, then turned and disappeared.

"Anchen, come inside," Mom said quietly from behind me.

Dad strode into the house and yanked open the door for my mother and me. Mom poured hot coffee and my parents sat down at the dining room table. I stood and stared at them.

Dad dumped some coffee into his saucer and slurped it, as he did every morning. He loved his coffee hot. Very hot. Moments later, he stood up and paced up and down the room. Up and down. He stopped and stared out the window. In his usual matter-of-fact voice he said, "Shep is dead."

I gasped and felt my heart pound, trying to escape my pajamas. "Dead?" Gone? I began to cry and scream, "NO! NO!" My best friend! How could I go on without him? I raced into my mother's arms and she pulled me onto her lap. I buried my head into her shoulder.

Dad yanked his chair back, scowled at Mom, and clenched his jaw and fists. "Anna, put her down. She's too old to sit on your lap! She needs to learn to be strong."

I gasped, then froze. Why was he so angry at Mom and me?

My mother held on to me and I saw tears in her eyes. Even though I was only nine, I wanted to protect her. I didn't want her to get into trouble because of me. Without a word I slid down Mom's lap and got up, standing stiff and straight, my head erect. I marched to my bedroom, and without a sound, I shut the door behind me. I slipped onto my bed and buried my face into my feather pillow, trying to hold back the silent sobs.

Moments later I heard the front door slam, and I knew Dad had left.

What had I done wrong? I could never do anything right for him. And I couldn't predict when his anger would crush my heart. Sometimes he would lash out and throw things at me. Then sometimes I'd do the same thing as I had done before, and he was kind and understanding. Why? Why? Oh, no, I had cried. I'd been weak. The words, "You have to be strong. You have to be strong," kept *flashing in front of me. It seemed that was all I ever heard from Dad. When was it my turn to just be me?*

Even then I knew there was something wrong with my dad. Sometimes I would hear him scream in the middle of the night, hear him pace up and down in the hall. Then the next day he would disappear and not speak to us for a day.

A few hours later, while sitting at the kitchen table, pretending to do my homework, I heard a truck drive up in the front yard. I jumped up and ran to the open window. Mr. Kehler, our neighbor from a half mile away, jumped off the runner of the giant Ford truck and slammed the door behind him. Cowboy hat in hand, he strode toward my father, who stood on the cement path just outside the porch. I hid behind the silk curtain so my dad wouldn't notice me watching.

"Afternoon Chnals," Mr. Kehler said, extending his hand. "You found your dog?"

My heart began to race. What did he mean? Found Shep? Was he still alive?

Dad nodded and shook his hand. "Found him by the garage this morning. You know who did it?" His voice was strained.

Mr. Kehler stepped back and glanced around. "Yeah. It was Mr. Bach. Yesterday evening."

"The one who lives on the way to town?"

"Yeah. I talked to one of his neighbors this morning. Said he saw him do it."

Dad's voice began to rise. "The man's insane! Why would he shoot my dog? Shep was always a good dog." I saw his face soften. "My daughter loved that dog. She's very upset."

Mr. Kehler pulled out a cigarette and lit it, puffed on it, and blew out a cloud of smoke. "Sorry Chnals. Says the wolves have been eating his calves. Says he's seen your dog run with the pack of wolves before. Thought he was one of them."

I covered my face with my hands and ran back into my bedroom. Shep. Oh, Shep. I knew now for sure he was dead.
Later I thought, at least he got to run with the wolves.

That evening without a word about the morning, Dad settled down on the leather sofa next to me. "Anchen, do you want me to continue my story about Russia? About the time we all voted to see if we would leave or fight?"

I was so relieved Dad wasn't mad at me anymore, that I quickly nodded my head. "Yes Daddy. Yes." I moved closer to him.

"Well, that night we had to vote," he said.

"Did you vote too?" I asked.

"No, only the head of each household got to vote."

"You mean Oma didn't get to vote? Why not?" I knew my mother always went to vote when Canada had elections.

Dad frowned. "That's just the way it was done in those days."

CHNALS

Feb. 7, 1918, dusk. One of the three churches in the Tereker Settlement. Men voting whether to leave or stay and fight.

At four o'clock, Chnals stole into the front door of the house. After helping the men from the village rally the cattle and most of the horses, he had watched them disappear down the muddy clay road. He swallowed hard. His life, his security, had disappeared down the road too, he thought.

Just then he saw Gerhard slip out of the kitchen to their room, his hands covering his face. Poor Gerhard. He was probably hiding in their bedroom.

"No, I'm not going to take that!" he heard his sister Sara yell at someone in the kitchen. "You just want me to take that picture because Grandma made it. That's because you're her favorite!"

Helena stomped out of the kitchen with a jar of pickles, her jaw set, and glared at Chnals. She headed to the dining room table. Oh, oh. His sisters were too busy arguing to notice Mama nod at Papa. As he hurried to the front door, he stopped near Chnals but didn't acknowledge him. Then he pulled on his leather jacket and boots.

"Can I come?" Chnals whispered.

Papa stared at him. "You know you're too young. Men over eighteen can come, but only the head of each household can vote. You stay here and take care of the others."

Chnals hung his head. It wasn't fair. Papa expected him to be as responsible as any of the men in the villages, but he had none of the privileges. He whirled around, held his head high and strode toward his room.

"Wait," Papa called after him. "You're right. You're almost thirteen and it's time for you to be with the men. Hard times are coming." Papa headed out the door with Chnals's favorite cap and jacket in his hand. "So are you coming?"

Chnals turned and dashed out of the house after Papa, and toward the barn. Together they saddled up Prinz, the big black horse Papa always rode. Without a word he jumped onto Prinz. He pulled Chnals into the saddle behind him, and they galloped down the driveway onto the road toward the church.

Several other horses clopped along in the muddy grooves on

the road. The men nodded to each other as they met, but did not speak. There were three churches in all for the seventeen villages, but each congregation would vote on their own.

When they arrived at the church-yard, Chnals glanced at his father who sat tall in front of him. He pulled at the reigns. "Whoa," he said. They dismounted and tied Prinz to a wooden post next to the other horses.

Several young men with rifles in hand stood in the front yard, arguing among each other. Chnals recognized his best friend's brother, Jacob. He hurried toward the group and stopped at the edge of the band of men to listen. They didn't seem to notice him.

"We have to fight. The Tatar bandits will come and destroy and steal everything we have worked so hard for these last seventeen years." Peter, a tall, stocky young man standing on a large rock, raised his rifle and shouted to the others. Several others raised their rifles and fists and cheered.

"Yes, they'll kill us all if we run and they catch us. We must fight to the death and protect our families," Abram yelled.

"That's suicide," Jacob yelled back. "Are you all crazy? Our only chance to survive is to leave and hide, and pray that God saves us."

"Coward!" another young man in a dark green jacket called out. The group raised their rifles again and cheered.

The large wooden church door nearby squeaked open. The light shone through the door and revealed a slender, middle-aged, man standing tall in the doorway. Oh, oh. Ohm Franz, the minister. His brow was furrowed and his eyes narrowed as he strode toward them. He clenched his fists. "Quiet. Get inside. It's time to talk and then vote." His voice was cold as steel.

The men lowered their rifles and bowed their heads. They began to follow Ohm Franz toward the church, still holding their rifles.

Ohm Franz wheeled around and stopped. "Guns don't belong in the church. Leave them outside." The men stood them up against the wall and quietly filed into the church.

Chnals jumped as he felt someone touch his shoulder. He swung around and saw Papa standing next to him. "You shouldn't be listening to those men. They are young and not in their right heads." He hurried Chnals up the steps and into the simple brick and clay church.

Inside, men, young and old, sat on rows of straight wooden benches. Some were bowed in prayer. Others sat, faces white and drawn, whispering to each other. The old men had clustered together on one side of the church and were reading their Bibles. The young men who had just entered took off their caps, and, still mumbling to each other, slid into the back benches.

A few of Chnals's friends had come with their fathers and brothers. Chnals and Papa sat down beside them. The boys smiled at each other and Papa bent his head in prayer.

Minutes later a hushed silence fell over the group as Ohm Franz walked up the aisle to the pulpit. The first words he said were, "Let us pray." The congregation bowed their heads and Ohm Franz prayed for protection, guidance, and wisdom in making the right decision for their community and the families.

The villages had always practiced democracy and peace in all their affairs, and both Catherine the Great who had brought them here from Germany to teach the Russians how to farm, and her son, had respected their freedom to govern their villages as they wished. Until recently the Czar's army had protected them. But now? Anarchists ran the country, and most of the soldiers left to join the Russian White Army against the anarchists and Communist Red Army.

Ohm Franz read a scripture describing Moses and the Israelites leaving Egypt. Then he said, "Before we vote, it is time to listen to each other about whether we should stay or go."

Peter, the stocky young man, stood up and said, "We have worked too hard these last years to build miles and miles of canals so we can grow fruit and wheat. And then we have to dig them out every year! Our villages feed many thousands of people now. We are the bread-basket of southern Russia. We can't let the Tatars win. They will steal everything. Even Jesus wouldn't want us to do that. We need to stand up for ourselves and what we believe." Most of the young men nodded as Peter sat down. Jacob shook his head slowly and frowned.

An elderly man placed his hands on the top of the bench in front of him and slowly pulled himself to a standing position. His face and hands were wrinkled and his legs trembled. "It's not right to fight and kill people. Jesus says we must love our enemies, and to turn the other cheek. If we're to be true to our beliefs, we must not fight. Our only option is to leave." All the elderly men looked down at their folded hands and nodded.

The room began to buzz and the words grew more strident, then harsh, as words flew over words, loud, then piercing. Chnals wanted to run out the door. This was not the way his family settled arguments. He wanted to place his hands tightly over his ears and scream, "Stop it!" but he dared not say a word. He was much too young. No one would listen to him. Why didn't Ohm Franz do something? From the shouting, it was clear that the young men were winning. They would all fight and die.

Finally a middle-aged man of about forty, who had been sitting quietly in his seat, stood up and headed to the front of the church. When he reached the pulpit he grasped the edge so tightly his knuckles turned white. He stood for a moment, watching the group, then lifted his arms, the palms of his hands turned toward them. The crowd jerked to attention and gaped at him.

"All of you. Sit down and be silent," he commanded. "Listen to me."

Ohm Franz stood up beside him and the men hushed. "Robert. Please speak."

"Maria and I have four children. We have our parents here in Village #5, and our brothers and sisters and friends." He pointed at two of his brothers sitting on the front bench. Have we forgotten about all of them? Are our properties, our homes, our gold and silver more important to us than these? We all know what has happened to the villages in the south. Most of the people are dead. What good do these things do us if all the people we love are gone? Our only chance to survive and escape to freedom is to leave as fast as we can and hide."

Murmurs echoed through the church as Robert stumbled down from the podium toward his seat, his eyes filling with tears.

"Are we ready to vote?" Ohm Franz said quietly. He folded his hands in prayer and asked the Almighty for wisdom. For the right decision. Four men handed out the ballots to the head member of each household, and when all the members had voted, the men collected them in their hats, then sat down in the choir loft and counted them. Ohm Franz, with eyes closed and hands folded, sat next to them. For the first time since Chnals had arrived at the church, it was completely silent.

At last one of the men handed Ohm Franz a piece of paper. He glanced at it, then walked to the podium, his face blank and inscrutable. He faced the audience and stopped. Slowly he turned and gazed into all the men's faces as though searching each one's heart.

He took a deep breath and said, "We gather here at the church at six o'clock tomorrow morning to leave."

STORY 4

Escape from the Tereker Villages

ANNA

SATURDAY'S WERE ALWAYS *the same it seemed. Feed the chickens, clean the bedroom, and wash our new black Plymouth car, with my sister. My father insisted on a sparkling clean black car ready for church and Sunday family rides.*

"Stop. Stop!" I screamed as I slammed the front door of our car and sprinted away from the stream of water Lee directed at me. My jeans and cotton shirt dripped with water.

Lee roared with laughter and jumped up and down continuing to spray water at me.

Mom rushed out the front door of the house and yelled at us. "Stop it girls! Lee, you're getting her all wet. That water is cold. You're fourteen and she's only nine. You should know better."

Lee threw the hose into the long grass and stomped her foot. "Mom, it's not my fault. I told her to get out of the car but she wouldn't listen to me." She swiveled to face me and scowled. "I told you, I have work to do and I can't just stand around while you fiddle the time away. I saw you wipe the dashboard three or four

31

times." The truth was that I loved to listen to country music on the radio as I cleaned the inside of the car. It made work so much easier.

Well, that was Saturday. And then came Sunday. Early morning we dressed in our Sunday-best clothes and drove in our beautiful clean car to our small white country church. After Sunday school the teacher lined us up at the back of the church, ready to walk down the aisle. At the pulpit the minister called to us. "Come children. We have stories we want to tell you now."

We'd rush to the front of the church and sit down on the rug in a circle close to the piano. The minister called on the congregation for Freiwilliges *(spontaneous volunteer time)* to tell a story to us. Later, when I learned more about Native American story-telling to teach lessons and pass on history to the younger generations, the light finally flashed on in my dim brain. That was what the stories were all about!

My father often volunteered. He would stride up to the middle of the circle in his smart-looking dark suit, white shirt, and necktie, and sit down cross-legged. Oh no! What if he embarrassed me again? And I would scoot to the back of the group and stare down at the floor.

But the kids loved my dad and his stories about his escape from Russia. They would cheer and scramble closer to him.

"Has anyone here ever been told that they had to pack up and leave their home in twelve hours and never come back? To leave your friends and a lot of your family behind and everything you owned? Do you have any idea what you would do?"

I cringed and checked the other children. Their eyes popped out and they gasped. One boy, a little older than me, straightened and raised his hand. "Kind of. I think I did. My parents told my sister and me we would lose our farm. We had no money. All the cows had died."

I turned to him and wanted to ask why all the cows had died and what had happened to save the farm, but I didn't dare to interrupt to ask stupid questions.

"I'm sorry," my father said. He stretched his hand out to the boy and touched him gently on the shoulder. "Thank you for telling us." Looking each child in the eyes, he said "Always remember how lucky you are to live in a free country. Never let your freedoms go."

It was a refrain I would hear from him many, many times in my life.

Never let your freedoms go.

CHNALS

Feb. 9, 1918, Three a.m. At home.
Preparing to leave the Tereker Villages.

Chnals heard a soft knock on his bedroom door. He jerked awake. What time was it? He felt as though he had barely closed his eyes and dozed. Had something happened? He jumped out of bed, dashed to the door, and opened it.

Papa stood in the hall, the light from the living room lamp illuminating him, fully dressed in his everyday dark pants and jacket. Obviously he was ready to go. "It's three o'clock. We need to leave."

Chnals gasped, "Three o'clock?" *What? Why?* He felt his heart beat faster. "Is something wrong?"

Papa glanced at Gerhard still sound asleep in the bed. Raising his hand to his mouth, he whispered. "Don't wake up Gerhard. We need to leave. Maybe back to Ukraine."

"To Ukraine?" He knew Papa's parents lived somewhere in Ukraine about twelve hundred *werst* (kilometers) away, but he had never met them before. "But why? Aren't we coming back here as soon as the Tatars are gone?"

"*Shhh.* I don't know." Papa hesitated for a moment, then squared his jaw and stared at the dark window across the room. Moments later he cleared his throat and said, "Oma and Opa won't be coming with us in our group of wagons. We must go now and say goodbye to them." His voice was strained.

Chnals felt a sudden coldness drain into his chest. He swallowed hard. "What do you mean? They're not coming with us? Papa, they can't stay here! The Tatars will kill them!" Oh, oh, the words had come out louder than he had meant them to. He glanced at Gerhard, who shot up in bed and rubbed his eyes.

Papa motioned Chnals to come out in the hall. He closed the door behind them. "They'll have to leave with another group. People from their village will be heading south to Jangi Jurt and Petrowsk. We can't all go to Kasi Jurt and then to Chassow Jurt to get on the train. There's no place for all of us to hide when the Tatars come."

Tears sprang up in Chnals's eyes. Oma and Opa were like a second set of parents to them. And Mama… How could she leave her mother and father behind and not know what happened to them? He gulped and said, "When will we see them again?"

Papa turned his head and looked down the hall toward his and Mama's bedroom. Chnals could hear the catch in Papa's words as he said, "*Shh.* Be kind to your mother. Don't say anything to her. She's not taking it well. I need you to help me load the wagon."

Shaking, Chnals tiptoed back into his bedroom. Gerhard lay back down again, and covered his head with their wool blanket. He could hear Gerhard crying. But what could he tell him? Besides, Chnals didn't have time to sit and comfort him now. They had to leave. Gerhard too would have to learn to take care of himself and be strong. Yanking on the dark wool pants, dress shirt, jacket and black leather boots he had put out yesterday, he rushed out the door to the kitchen.

On the table lay a short list Mama and Papa had made of all the items to bring. He stared at it. That was it? How long could the nine of them survive on this? Besides, he had seen his mother's tummy grow over the last months. Even though Mama and Papa never spoke of it to the children, he knew what that meant. Soon there would be another mouth to feed.

He opened the small flour sack next to the list and checked inside. It smelled of peppermint and lavender soap. Odds and ends such as combs, scissors, soap, candles, matches and endless other small essentials filled about half the sack. On the wooden bench next to the table, where three of his sisters usually plunked down for meals, sat several boxes of salt pork, eggs, potatoes, flour with a bottle of yeast, cabbage and carrots, as well as a box of dishes and cutlery. Two cans of milk rested on the floor nearby. All he needed to do now was carry them to the wagon and make sure that each person in the family tucked their extra clothes into a sack and brought them along.

Mama hurried into the kitchen, eyes red, her long hair uncombed, gripping another flour sack bag. He knew what was in that bag! Late last night Chnals had seen his mother and father scurry around after everyone else was asleep. They were packing all their precious items...his mother's special jewelry, Papa's pocket watch, antiques from Germany, and many things made out of gold, and silver. And, of course, rubles. Lots and lots of rubles.

Suddenly his mind began to whirl. Were the precious items in that bag there to sell and trade to help them survive in case of emergency? *And what if the Tatars caught them?* They would steal not only the money, but everything else, even the food. And kill them! He shook his head. No, he couldn't think of that now. Papa was right. He had to be strong.

He nodded to Mama, not wanting to make eye contact in case he revealed that he knew the secret about Oma and Opa. "*Guten Morgen, Mama,*" he said as he grabbed a box and hoisted it onto his shoulder. He squared his shoulders and carried the box of salt pork out to the large four-wheeled wagon on the wet-packed clay and dirt driveway. Thank heaven it had stopped raining and the moon peeked out from behind the clouds. Papa grabbed the box and arranged it next to the three cans of water already on the wagon. He threw one of the dark quilted blankets over the cans and strode back into the house, probably to get the cans of milk. They were too heavy even for Chnals.

He ran inside to help Papa bring the rest of the boxes to the cart. Down the hall he could hear Sara and Justina squabble over something, probably about those three special things each of them could bring. That would be just like those stupid girls. It was time for them to grow up too!

About half an hour later, when all the boxes had been loaded, Chnals rushed into the barn to help Papa harness the two giant work horses that would pull the wagon. He stopped and gulped. All the other horses, except Papa's special black horse Prinz were gone. And the cows? Where were they? And then he remembered. The village men had come last night and taken them all to the meadow by the woods."

Papa grabbed the reins and led the horses out of the barn. He called back to Chnals, "Open the door to the chicken barn and let them out."

"They'll freeze!" he said more to himself than to Papa.

Papa cleared his throat. "They need to be free...just in case."

"Oh." Chnals gulped, then turned and rushed to the old shed and flung open the door. The chickens fluttered and squawked. He checked around. Brown eggs lay softly clothed by hay in the nests, probably still warm to the touch. He turned and shoved a large rock between the rickety door and unpainted wood shed, waved goodbye to the chickens, and ran to the wagon.

Papa hitched the horses to the wagon and climbed onto the back.

The girls staggered out of the house with their sacks. Papa hauled each one of the five girls onto the wagon and settled them into a special spot, then covered them with dark blankets. A moment later Chnals saw Mama yank Gerhard screaming out of the door.

"Shh." Papa's voice sounded harsh. "Be quiet! Not a sound till we get inside Oma and Opa's house."

Chnals turned and hurried to help his mother with Gerhard. Mama whispered to him, "Go back and check the house." He nodded his head. "Make sure the fire in the stove is out and you blow out the lamp."

After Mama and Gerhard were safely settled in the wagon, Chnals dashed back inside. One more time. Just in case. He looked around and touched the stove. Cold. He stopped inside the living room. The smell of roast chicken and fresh bread still lingered in the house. A lump rose in his throat as he looked around. Home! He swallowed hard. This was the place where he had always felt safe, felt loved. The place he could play and have fun. He could almost hear the laughter echo through the abandoned house.

His heart sank low into his stomach as he saw his favorite picture still on the wall. It was of the Caucasus Mountains with the whole family in the foreground on one of their outings. Under the picture and to the right, sat the hand-built rocker he had helped Grandpa whittle out of cherry wood. He touched it and his hand lingered on the smooth arm.

His eyes wandered to the big grandfather clock close to the door. A beloved family friend. Quiet. It was the first time in his life he had seen the pendulum still. His parents had dragged the clock all the way from Ukraine when they had first arrived here in 1903, full of hope, three years before he was born. At last Chnals turned to the book case next to the rocking chair and checked it. Yes, all his favorite books were still there. Except the 1892 German Martin Luther Bible. He gulped again. Of course. Mama had packed it. They would need it for comfort in the days to come.

"Chnals, where are you? We have to leave. *Schnell* (quick)!" Papa yelled from the yard.

In a moment his thoughts jumped back to the present. "I'm coming Papa," he called back. He turned down the last kerosene lamp and blew it out. Then he stopped and looked back again.

Just maybe...maybe...soon the villagers would all be back and everything would still be as it had been all his life. And he would see Oma and Opa and all his friends again. And feed the chickens...and go to school...

Yes. He had to believe. He had to have faith.

As he left, his eyes lit on the rack by the front door. His favorite cap still hung on the rack where he had left it last night when he and Papa got home from the church. Snatching it from the hook, he swung it onto his head and pulled it down a little in the front as he always did. He grabbed a heavy down jacket from the rack and yanked it on over his wool one. He glanced back one more time, then softly closed the door behind him.

"*Auf wiedersehen*," he whispered. *Until we meet again.*

The full moon blinked in and out through the clouds, casting a fleeting white light on the road. The wagon glugged down the muddy clay street toward Village #9 with Prinz tied securely to the back of it. The smell of decaying wet leaves almost made Chnals sneeze. Except for Chnals, all the children and Mama huddled under the dark blankets, quiet as the little mice that loved to softly squeak around in their kitchen at night. Danger! They must not be seen by invaders. Chnals sat tall next to Papa in the front of the wagon, on one of the water cans, in case Papa needed him to grab the reins. He could hear the sound of the mud on the wheels. *Plah, plah, plah.* And it lulled him into quietness.

As they passed the fields of grass and winter wheat, the years of his life began to unroll like a spool of thread on his mother's treadle sewing machine, faster and faster. So many memories. So many pictures in his mind. The countless days when he was young, that he and his friends helped Papa and the village men dig canals from the Sulag River to irrigate the acres and acres of fruit trees, sugar cane, wheat, and corn fields. Each of the villages had an artesian well, except for the three where gas and oil gushed out instead of water, and blew up as the men dug. The Tereker Settlement had sold oil to a Russian-English company for the last years.

The wagon rolled past the space near the country store in the orchard, where the villagers gathered each Friday to play flute, guitar, and violin, to fiddle away the dreary hours as they sang German folk songs and played lively games. The school. The church. The giant clump of trees and *Tamariske Strauch* (red blossomed shrubs) in which he and his friends had played hide-and-seek so many times. The muck of the swampy land.

Each of the villages had about thirty farms and an elementary school. The settlement also had a brick factory, a bank, a high school, a library, and a teacher's coop and college. What would happen to all that the settlers had created if they could never come back?

Out of the blue, Papa turned toward him and muttered, "Here Chnals. You take the reins." Chnals jerked to attention, stood up, and grabbed the reins from his father. Was something wrong? Chnals turned just a little to check on him. Papa leaned back and stared out into the distance. His hand shook as he brushed his eyes with his jacket sleeve. Chnals gulped. Tears. Papa...strongest of all strong men. But of course! He was remembering too. Chnals felt the wetness well up in his own eyes, but he blinked the tears away. Papa mustn't see that he had noticed.

But what was his father remembering? Chnals clucked at the horses and glanced around. Where were they? The Fishery that the village men had built loomed in the distance to their left. And the pungent odor of fish hung in the air as they neared. He knew how many hours Papa had worked with neighbors and friends to catch fish and clean them for all their villages and trade them along with flour, to the Muslim villages near them. There had always been fish sandwiches for lunch and lobster galore for dinner. Ugh! He was getting sick of eating fish and lobster.

About a mile down the road Papa grabbed the reins again and slapped them on the horses' flanks to hurry them along. Soon after, they passed the High School, then the Teachers College, and the Apothecary. Then the brick making factory.

As they neared the Caspian Sea his mind flitted back to the many times he and his friends had swung on the tall trees next to the shore, had screamed with laughter, and jumped out into the sea. Splash! The many times they had gone swimming in the ice cold water.

As they drove, the clouds disappeared and the moon glistened on the wet weather-worn board at the side of the road with the words Village 9 carved into it. He could make out the many acres of orchards around them, now with barren branches. Apples, pears, peaches, cherries, and apricots. Apricots. His favorite fruit, ripe on the tree. He felt his face flush as he remembered the time he and his friends had climbed those trees and snuck apricots out of his grandparent's orchard after dark. Thank heaven they had never found out...or had they? Oma packed several boxes of apricots each year and smiled as she said, "Chnals. Why don't you share these with your friends?"

Tears filled his eyes again. If only.

Just one more time...

Shaking, he slid to the wagon floor, covering himself with a blanket. They would be at Oma and Opa's house soon.

Clop, clop. Clop, clop. Clop, clop.

Minutes later he felt the wagon slow down and veer to the right.

"Whoa!" Papa called out. The horses whinnied and the wagon lurched to a stop.

Chnals threw off his blanket. There was Grandpa Schmidt standing at the front door to the one-story brick-and-clay house. The lantern light flickered in his hand, illuminating the mud and gravel walk between them.

The girls began to chatter as they tossed their blankets aside.

"*Shhh.* Not a word," Papa said in his most threatening voice.

Katarina, Jus, and Sara jumped out of the wagon and raced to Opa. Helena slipped down from the back and quietly followed, head bent, arms dangling to the side. Chnals grabbed the reins and Papa extended his hand to help Mama, two year old Maria, and Gerhard down onto the walk. Papa tied the horses to the post and Chnals followed the others, mud slopping on his shoes.

"Where's Oma?" Helena whispered to Opa as she stepped on the porch next to him.

Without a word he motioned to the door.

The door creaked open and there in the shadows stood Oma, dressed in a long dark winter dress, grey-brown hair tied up in a large knot. The children ran inside and Mama folded into Oma's arms. They kissed each other on the cheeks as was the custom, then both held on to the other for what seemed like hours.

Oma let go and stepped inside, motioning with her hand. "Come, come children. You need a bite to eat before you go."

Inside, the house smelled of pork *Greven* (chitlins) and fried potatoes. As on all their visits, the long wooden table was set for everyone. His brother and sisters dashed to the table and sat in their usual spots, babbling on about something. Chnals couldn't care less about what they were saying. Girl stuff. Instead of joining them, he hung around close to the kitchen door in case Papa came in and needed a hand. Of course he was fooling himself. This way he could hear what Mama and Oma were talking about.

Mama gasped as she walked into the kitchen. "Why aren't you ready to leave?" Mama's whisper was tight and strained.

"We don't know yet...when. Many have gone already."

Chnals's jaw dropped. What? Oma and Opa weren't leaving this morning?

Mama stared at Oma. "What do you mean? You have to go now!" Mama's voice rose.

"Yes, yes, we know. It's just that the people here that we will travel with aren't ready yet. They think maybe if they wait..." Oma hurried to the stove and tossed a mixture of milk and eggs into an old cast iron pan already sizzling with pork fat.

"What's the matter with them? Don't they know the Tatars are coming down the mountains right now?"

Oma stirred the eggs and milk over and over again. Her eyes never left the pan. He heard a muffled cry coming from the table. His head snapped around. Oh no! Helena's eyes were large and her jaw wide open. She had heard!

At that moment Opa strode into the room, his hands on his

hips, his brow furrowed. He stepped between Oma and Mama. "It's time to eat," he said, his voice loud and stern. Mama headed for the table, and head bowed, sat down next to Helena. Oma kept stirring the eggs...

Minutes later the front door creaked open and Papa marched into the kitchen, his pants spattered with sticky clay.

Mama grabbed her cloth napkin, ran over to Papa, and wiped the wet mud. "What happened? Are you okay?"

"Oh it's nothing. Those *dumkopf* horses!" he muttered, sitting down at the table next to Mama.

Oma scooped the eggs and fried potatoes into a large, flowery ceramic bowl and joined them with a plate of fresh bread. After everyone was served, they said grace in unison as they did at each meal. *Vater segne diese Speise. Uns zum kraft und dier zum Preise. Amen.* They dug in and ate in silence like good German children. Chnals noticed Mama stir the food on her plate but rarely lift the fork to her mouth.

Opa and Papa talked of how well the winter wheat looked and how many bushels per acre it should yield in spring. And how they would be back soon to sow the wheat for the second crop of the year, and work in the Fishery, and make cheese.

About an hour later Grandpa pulled his pocket watch out of his wool pants pocket. He glanced at it and stood up. "It's time." He motioned to Mama and Papa to follow him. They hurried down the hall.

Oma stayed behind with the children for a few minutes, then said, "We'll be back soon. You need to get ready to head to the church now." She followed the others to one of the empty bedrooms.

Chnals stared at the half-eaten eggs on his plate, and the mush in his stomach wanted to rise and spew out onto his now empty life.

As the girls struggled out the door, they shoved each other toward the wagon parked next to the barn. Helena suddenly twisted around, almost collapsing into the mud. Chnals could hear her cry as she bent her head and rushed back toward the house. But of course. Oma! Helena had always been Oma's favorite, and they were as close as any mother and daughter.

Oma hurried from the porch and ran toward her. "Helena! Helena! Come here. It's okay." Helena buried her head into Oma's chest, weeping and holding on to her. She held her tight and Chnals could tell Oma was crying by the way she trembled as she stroked Helena's long brown hair. "It's okay. It's okay. We'll see you again very soon."

Chnals gasped as he saw Papa stride toward Helena and yank her toward him. But Helena held so tight to Oma's long dress that she stumbled to the wet ground. Without a word, Papa picked Helena up and rushed her to the wagon. Moments later he yelled at the horses and they galloped away without another word.

Chnals bowed his head. *You have to be strong. You have to be strong.* The words kept skipping through his mind. Why? Why had she cried? Didn't Helena know that she should never show her real feelings? Then his mind turned blank. No more thinking. No more wishing. It was like the eggs in the frying pan. No, his world had turned from liquid into mush. No more wishing. No more dreaming of a wonderful future. Eggs boiled and turned to mush. So much like their lives. Liquid, now turned to solid. All their choices…gone.

STORY 5
Traveling to Kasi Jurt

ANNA

SO OKAY. IT *was Sunday. A day of rest. Right? Not really. Not if you lived on a farm. After church we had roast rooster and garden potatoes at my Grandpa and the auntie's farm. And when we came home it was time to feed the chickens, and milk the cows..., and feed the horses some hay..., and throw slop into the bin for the pigs, and...and...and....*

But my mind kept wandering back to my father's story at church. Wow, that was the wrong place to end the last story, I thought! I was peeved at my dad. How dare he leave me stranded there in Russia? I knew he had survived, but how about his Oma and Opa? My great-grandparents. I had never met them. Did they live? And what had happened to all of them after they left their home?

I had to find a way to convince my dad, in just the right way, to tell me the rest of the story, so he didn't get mad at me for asking stupid questions. Well, I knew if I was extra good and I brought a paper from school with an A on it on Monday, he would be open. And then, maybe if I sat on the sofa next to him that night and asked. Yes. That would work.

I slept very little during the night, planning Monday's moves. That next evening, I sidled up to Dad, still in his overalls, sitting on the brown leather sofa in the living room. I knew it was almost time for me to go to bed. "Dad, look!" *I said. I shoved a piece of brownish tan paper filled with arithmetic figures into his hand. On the top in red ink the teacher had put a giant A+ and had scribbled a sentence below it.* "Good job, Anna." *it read.*

My dad smiled a big smile and tousled my brown hair. I snuggled a little closer. "So what did you learn in school today?" *he asked.*

"History," *I said.* "The history of the world. We even talked about Russia." *Note, I was careful not to refer to Russia as the Soviet Union.* "You told me a while ago that you lived near the Muslim villages in the south. You said you would tell me about the different kinds of Muslims." *I looked up into his eyes.* "I could tell everyone at school about that during history class."

Dad's face mellowed and he gazed out toward the dark window. "That was a long time ago. I was only twelve."

I nodded, hoping he would continue. My sister Lee sat in the dining room at the table doing her homework, and I noticed her head turn a little toward us. I figured she wanted to hear the story too, but had to pretend she didn't care, now that she was a teenager.

"We lived in what you now call Dagestan, near the mouth of the Sulag River on the Caspian Sea, and close to the northern Caucasus Mountains." *He rose and hurried to the oak desk in the living room, opened a large drawer, and pulled out some papers.* "See, here is the map." *He unfolded the sheet of paper.* "You can show it to the class tomorrow." *Dad handed it to me and sat down again, pointing out where they had lived.*

My eyes turned big. "Really? You lived there?"

"Yes. There were three kinds of Muslims that lived near us. They were called Tatars in those days. There were the Mountain Tatars, the Tschetschenzen. They were very poor and very war-like. The *young men would come down and rob from the German villages. Then they'd shoot up the towns and steal our best horses."*

My mother peeked around the door from the kitchen. She looked at Dad and frowned.

He stopped for a moment, then said, "As long as the Czar's soldiers were around, they protected us. We were okay. But when the revolution started. Well, I told you about that."

I nodded my head again. I wanted to say we had covered that already and let's get on with the story, but I clamped down my lips tight and said nothing.

"Then there were some villages to the south of us that we got along with, but they didn't have much. They were called the Rogaier people. The men often worked for us. We paid them and they helped us build the canals and work the land." He hesitated and his voice faltered. He looked out to the dark window again. By now I knew what that meant. He was remembering something important.

I saw Lee creep into the living room with her Nancy Drew book from the school library, and sit down in Mom's rocker. She hid her face in her book.

"And then there was a third group that lived in the villages east of us." Dad stopped again, then cleared his throat. "The Kumeken people were our friends, and the people we traded with. They were quite rich. They sold us household things like cutlery and dishes, and we sold them flour and fruit.

You know, all the people were Muslims and believed in Mohammed instead of Jesus, but each group was very different. They had their own languages and customs. It was a little bit like here in Manitoba. Like our German towns and French and Ukrainian towns around us."

I knew about that. After all, I had some French speaking friends in a nearby town.

"Did they speak German?"

A smile crossed his face. "No. No. Most of them spoke no Russian and of course no German. Just their own Turkish dialect. The head of the village spoke a little Russian and he even sent his son Abdul to live with Ohm Franz so he could go to our schools and learn."

"He lived in your village?" Wow! That was weird. But then I remembered one of the boys at my country school who had just moved here from Mexico. He spoke no English, and for lunch he ate onion and butter sandwiches. His jeans were often torn. My dad and mom told my sister and me to be especially nice to him, and not make him feel different.

Dad nodded his head. "Yes, he came with us that day when we had to leave our villages."

By this time I had almost forgotten about all the plans I had made last night to ask Dad to continue his story. My mind jolted back. Now was the time to pop the question. Quick, before Mom put me to bed. I sat up taller and folded my hands.

"Dad, yesterday at church you told the story—. What happened after you left your Oma and Opa's place?"

Dad seemed to check my face, then sat up taller, just like me. He nodded. "Yes. Yes. I should have told you. I just didn't have time in church yesterday. And then I forgot." He settled back into the sofa. "After we left Oma and Opa's house, lots of people gathered at the church. We had to all be very quiet in case the Tatars had sent out a guard who might hear us."

CHNALS

February 9, 1918, six a.m. Travelling to Kasi Jurt.

An eerie silence covered the village. Even the wind seemed to know not to speak. And the moon hid in darkness behind the heavy clouds bearing down on the land.

As before, Chnals sat up in the front of the wagon near Papa. He felt the goose bumps on his arms rise as he stared at the long line of wagons near the church, stretching out until it faded into black.

"What's going to happen?" Chnals whispered.

"Be quiet," Papa said in a gruff but low voice. "No talking. I'll tell you later. When we're safe."

Chnals leaned back on one of the water cans and tried to relax, but his body was still on full alert. His insides jumped as he heard a frog croak out in its high, shrill, voice. For a moment he wanted to yell out, "*Shh.*" But of course he didn't. He knew better. Thank goodness, at least the masses of mosquitoes that usually swarmed the wagon were still asleep.

"Number Sixteen," Oberschultz (Mayor) Peters called out from the steps of the church. Papa slapped the reins on the horses and the cart lunged forward again, right behind Wagon Fifteen and onto the road. There were thirty homes in Konstantinowka and each household had been given a number.

Moments later Wagon Seventeen lined up behind them. From what Chnals could see, everyone except the driver was covered in dark blankets, just like Mama and his brother and sisters. Obviously everything had been carefully arranged and organized among all the families of the village late last evening. According to Oberschultz Peters, they should all be well on the road and into the woods before the sun came up and the Mountain Tatars galloped into town.

As they moved forward onto the wet clay road, he felt the wheels jolt into the deep ruts. Little Maria screamed out. "Quiet," Mama whispered. Under the blankets he could see Mama's legs rock back and forth. Maria whimpered, but then the world went back to the quiet of the night.

Thoughts piled on thoughts like the many-layered pile of straw and manure behind their barn. What about Oma and Opa and all his friends? And would the people at Kasi Jurt be willing to let them hide there until the Mountain Tatars were gone, and they could all go home again? Chnals took some deep breathes and tried hard not to think. Now was not the time to fall apart. He gripped onto the cold, metal, water can so tightly he was sure his hand had turned white. He could hear the clopping of horses' hooves and the creak of wagon wheels ahead of him.

Kasi Jurt lay only ten *werst* (about seven miles) southeast of their villages, and now that they were on the road, the trip would not take long. They passed the teachers college, the credit union, and the book binding shop behind the library. As they neared the rickety wooden bridge spanning the Talma Canal that all the villagers had worked so hard to build, he took a deep breath. Miles and miles of canals, watered their sixty seven thousand acres of land and kept the Talma river from flooding each spring and creating months of swamps. The area had been a mosquito breeding ground. In the early days, hundreds of the settlers had died of typhus and malaria. Finally, within the last few years, diseases had become rare and the fields fertile and green year round. Now this.

The loose planks of the bridge groaned as the wheels of the wagon ahead of them, with its heavy load, rolled slowly across. Then it was their turn. It was a good thing the horses knew where to go even in the dark.

Papa pulled the reins and the horses slowed to a walk. Suddenly Prinz, tied to the back of the wagon, stumbled on a board and vaulted to the side of the bridge. Prinz rose on his hind legs and screamed into the dark. The wagon jerked back and forth, then stopped. He heard gasps from under the blankets and the cans tumbled and rolled to the side of the wagon. Oh no! The milk! Chnals reached for the can just as Papa thrust the reins into his hands and stumbled to the back of the wagon. Too late.

"Prinz!... Prinz! Stop!!!" Papa's voice split the silence.

"Helena!" Chnals yelled. "The milk!" Helena threw off her blanket and grabbed the milk can as it hurtled by. The lid burst open and milk spilled onto her shoes. She hauled it upright and covered the top again. Wow, that had been too close! They would need that milk to drink, to cook with, and make cottage cheese.

The horses behind them whinnied and swung off the road, then jolted to a halt. Papa jumped out of the wagon. "Whoa. Quiet now," he commanded in his calmest voice. As soon as Prinz heard Papa, he seemed to relax. Chnals had always known that Prinz was Papa's best friend. Maybe even more like a son. The ever-obedient Prinz settled down enough for Papa to untie him and lead him across the bridge. Minutes later, Chnals coaxed the two work horses pulling the wagon, over the bridge. He yanked the rein and they veered to the right, then stopped in the long, wet grass.

Mr. Dueck jumped out from the wagon behind theirs and ran across the bridge, calling out, "Mr. Unger. Are you okay?"

Papa, still leading Prinz, called back, "Yes, yes. He's just scared. He doesn't like to leave home like this. He knows there's something wrong." Papa laughed a bit, probably to lessen the tensions now spreading like wildfires around them all.

The two men talked for a few minutes as the other wagons rumbled past them. Then all was quiet again. Papa jumped up onto Prinz and rode back toward him. "You follow Mr. Dueck," he commanded. "I'll be right behind you."

Chnals's jaw dropped, but he nodded. Then he took a deep breath. It was up to him now. Part of him felt proud that Papa trusted him. But what if he failed? The family's lives were in his hands. He straightened and clucked to the horses, then slapped the reins against their flanks. He was sure his body shook so hard the horses would feel it through the reigns. Was Papa right that the horses could tell they were all in danger?

As the wagon train wound toward the Sulag River, the darkness began to lift. They had better hurry! At the river-bank, he gazed to the west. Mount Elbrus. The highest mountain in the Caucasus. Each morning on his way to school, he would check the mountain and think of its beauty. How everlasting, never changing. Even the snow on the top never disappeared. He swallowed hard. Yes, this was home. The only home he had ever known. He blinked hard and straightened. They would be back soon.

Minutes later, the wagons veered to the west and followed the river into the birch and pine forest toward Kasi Jurt. As the last wagons faded into the dense trees, Chnals breathed a long sigh and almost dropped the reins. Even the horses seemed to relax and slow down. They were all safe.

About a half hour later, he noticed the sun begin to spread its wings in the sky like the eagles he so often came to watch near the river. The people in the wagons, now visible, had discarded their dark blankets, and he heard them cheering as they began their ascent from the valley to the green hills. His sisters jerked the blankets aside and began to chatter. Little Maria started to cry and Mama pulled her closer into her arms. Mama dipped her hand into her pocket and gave Maria a sugar cookie. She stuffed it into her mouth, and Chnals could hear the smacking and munching all the way to the front of the wagon. He suddenly felt hungry.

As the wagons burst out of the forest onto the top of the hill, the smell of smoke stung his nostrils. Were the forests burning? Why? Fires were very unlikely in winter, and the rainy season.

Rows of wagons lined up ahead of them. Chnals gasped as several men dashed to the flat, open meadow on the hill, overlooking the Tereker Settlement. What was going on? Plumes of smoke curled up and blew toward them, almost obscuring the sun. In a panic he parked the wagon next to the others and jumped out. Papa galloped up behind him and secured Prinz to the back of the wagon. Together they rushed to join the other men. The women and children hurried behind them. As one body, they all dropped their jaws and stared to the east.

Suddenly he heard ear-shattering screams such as he had never heard before. Young men yelled and raised their fists. Women cried and herded their children together like young calves threatened by wolves. Old men slouched to the ground, weeping and praying, as if the end of the world predicted in the Bible had finally come.

His heart thumped shut, and his head went numb. Stunned, Chnals stood and watched for what seemed a long, long time, as the villages below them burned and the smoke rose to the sky. He felt as though he were sitting at a vast distance from there, on top of Mt. Elbrus.

Home? Gone. They could never return.

A few days earlier, his mother had cried and said they should never have left Ukraine in 1903.That God had never meant for them to live here in Dagestan. The settlers should have known better than to buy this forsaken land from that wealthy feudal lord in 1901.But Papa had reminded her that the last eight years had brought harvests of fruit, grain, and hay unparalleled in the area. They had ground the wheat into flour, and their villages had become the bread basket for southern Russia. They had all become wealthy farmers.

Now this.

Then he heard someone weep next to him. Chnals turned and saw his mother and Helena doubled over in pain, tears streaming down their cheeks.

In an instant he remembered. Oma and Opa. Had they left on time? He folded his hands and fell down on his knees.

God. Please, please, keep them safe.

ANNA

At this point in the story my father started to fidget. Then suddenly he exploded into a rage, throwing the book he had been reading before he told me the story about leaving for Kasi Jurt. It crashed against the living room wall across from us. I stared and pressed myself back into the sofa. What had happened? Moments later he stormed out of the house. Through the living room window, I glimpsed him rush toward the yard light, then disappear into the darkness.

My mother said nothing, but her face was long and drawn. She looked very, very sad. "Anna, it's time for bed," she said softly.

I refused to budge. What had happened? I stared up at her. "Mom. What's wrong? Where did Dad go?" I felt scared and sick to my stomach. She didn't answer. But why was he so angry? Had I done something terribly wrong by asking him to tell me a story about Russia?

"It's okay," she replied at last as she hurried me to my room.

Long after we were all in bed, I heard the front door open and close. Then nothing. That night I jerked awake to a horrible scream from my parents' bedroom, next to mine. Dad! I froze. After that I heard his footsteps in the hall. Back and forth. Back and forth.

I began to shake.

At last I heard my mother come out and say, "Chnals. You know you shouldn't talk about that time in Russia. It just makes it worse. Forget about what happened! You can't do anything about that now."

Oh, oh. It was my fault. I had asked him to tell me the story of their escape from the village. I covered my head with my blanket and quietly sobbed into my pillow. I slept very little that night. The next morning, I pretended to be my cheerful self. My parents said nothing. I knew by now that they never spoke of feelings and personal stuff to us.

After school, my sister and I mounted Johnny, the white race horse Dad had bought for us, and galloped the three miles home. Had my sister Lee heard Dad during the night? I dared not ask. Lee led Johnny to the pasture, took off his saddle, and released him into the meadow with the other horses. I ran into the house to get the peanut butter cookies and milk Mom always set out for us after school. I turned on my favorite afterschool radio program "The Lone Ranger." But my mind kept returning to yesterday.

"Quick. Can you help me?" Mom called out from the porch. Still in my school clothes, I raced through the kitchen and opened the front door.

I gasped when I saw her."Mom, what are you doing?" She stood in front of me with a giant cardboard box, her hands plastered with gunk. The box jiggled back and forth as if she carried a running motor inside.

Then I heard a noise. "Oink. Oink!" And I knew the answer to my question.

"Oh, goody!" I literally jumped with joy and held the door open wide until Mom and the box stumbled into the kitchen, and then the dining room. She placed it in a corner on the wood floor. I ran to the box and peeked inside. "Piggies!" I yelled.

Three tiny piglets lay on the straw, rooting around with their snouts, obviously looking for milk. I stroked their little heads and they tried to suck my fingers. Mama turned and hurried to the kitchen. Moments later, the refrigerator door slammed shut. I knew what she was going to do. Feeding little piggies was not a novel experience at our house.

"Mom, can I help? Please?" I called after her.

"Go get the nipples and bottles. You know where they are." I heard some pots rattle.

I rushed to the kitchen and pulled the stepstool to the closet next to the window, swung it open, and jumped onto the stool. I tugged down three bottles and nipples, then gave them to my mother, who stood waiting next to me. She filled them with milk and placed them in a pan of hot water on the counter.

"What happened to mama pig?" I asked. I clenched my jaw. I wished . . . hoped . . . she hadn't died like one of the other mama pigs a few months ago.

She took each bottle, shook it, and squirted some milk on her wrist. "Mama pig had too many little ones. She couldn't feed them all."

"Really?" I said, amazed that something like that could happen. "How many piggies did she have?" I had seen lots of them in my short life, but my parents had never allowed me to watch them being born. Here's a secret I never told them, but I had snuck into the barn once to check out the procedure. Yuck!

"Fourteen little ones." Mom said as she handed one of the bottles to me. "Here. Let's go. They need some food." She nodded toward the bottle on the counter and I grabbed the last one.

I followed her into the dining room and sat down on one of the carved oak chairs near the table. I smoothed my jeans and waited. Mom placed a towel on my lap, then grabbed a squiggling piglet from the box and handed it to me, his or maybe her, little eyes barely open. I placed the nipple into its mouth, and it slurped and slurped till all the milk was gone. Moments later, it was fast asleep on my lap. Gently I placed it back in the box. It squirmed a bit, snorted, then fell asleep again.

"Where is Dad?" I whispered to Mom so as not to wake the piggies.

My mother swallowed hard and glanced at me. She grabbed the empty bottles and hurried back to the kitchen. "He'll be home soon, He went to seed some corn for the cows at the other land." That meant he had been gone since early morning, because our second quarter of land was about three miles away.

Okay, here is something most people don't know. Newborn piglets need to eat every two hours, night and day. So later that evening, just before bed, there I was again. A piglet on my lap. Lee fed number two, and Mom fed number three.

At nine o'clock the lights of the tractor shone in through the living room window. Oh, oh. Dad was home. I gulped down my fear. Would he still be angry at me? About ten minutes later he burst through the outside door to the kitchen and slammed it behind him. Lee and I huddled down in our chairs, holding tight to our little piggies.

"Where's dinner?" he called into the dining room. My mother rushed out to the kitchen and I heard the rattle of dishes and cutlery. No one said a word, but I knew Mom stayed with him till he finished dinner. She always did. I saw him slip into their bedroom. Then all was quiet. He did not speak to any of us for almost a week. Actually this had happened several times before, and would again. At the time we had no idea when or what would trigger his rage or silence.

Today my father's condition would be called PTSD (Post-Traumatic Stress Disorder), but in those days no one knew, and no one spoke about it. I walked on glass shards throughout much of my early years, never knowing when the monster in Dad would erupt. He could be so loving and kind and then . . . . At the time I just thought he was an angry man and that I was to blame. I had done something wrong again, although I had no idea what. I didn't understand him until many years later, when I studied psychology in college.

STORY 6
Arrival in Kasi Jurt

ANNA

MOST YEARS, ON *a Sunday afternoon in August, the family would congregate at my grandfather's house to celebrate the family's escape to freedom. As a kid, I called it Thanksgiving Day Number One. (Thanksgiving Day Number Two was the usual country-wide celebration in October for our harvest and blessings.)*

Each family member told stories about their escape from Russia, as they remembered them. Besides my grandfather, my dad, who had been eighteen at the time, and Aunt Helena, twenty-one, were the oldest and therefore thought to have the most accurate memories, although Aunt Helena remained quiet most of the time. My grandmother had passed away in her fifties of a heart attack, before I was born.

Because August was often hot, humid, and sunny, the cousins, uncles, and aunts, and of course Grandpa, gathered in an open, giant shed set up with tables and chairs for the occasion. All the machinery such as tractors, combines, and plows, had been removed and towed to the back of the building.

We would have our usual dinner, varenika *with cream gravy, and for dessert, we each got a giant-sized* perisky *(baked fruit pocket). After dinner we removed the tables and circled the chairs for the stories. The aunties, chattering and laughing, usually chose the subject.*

Each year, as the storytelling grew to a close, my father would stand up tall next to Grandpa, and would give us the talk: "Children, you have no idea how lucky you are to live in a free country. Never, never, let your freedoms go. Don't let your fears rule you. Remember, God will go with you, regardless of where you are."

To this day these words pierce my mind like sharpened arrows at the most unexpected times, like right now, as I watch so many of the Ukrainian people run in terror for their and their families' lives.

One August when I was fourteen years old, the older family members spoke of what had happened after watching the Tereker Villages burn.

CHNALS

Arriving at Kasi Jurt

After the sound of weeping and the cries of sorrow had finally stopped, a death-like silence covered the wagon train. Except for an occasional whimper from his sisters, Chnals heard only the creak and groan of the wagons as they headed south up another hill toward Kasi Jurt. Looking back, he could see the trails of smoke rising from the villages and circling in the air. The smell of burning wood and smoldering clay bricks still stung his throat.

Before settling down on the floor of the wagon, Chnals glanced around to check on the others. Helena sat behind him, holding her arms around her buckled legs, her head bent to her knees. Mama cradled little Maria in her arms and rocked her back and forth, silent tears still streaming down her face. Not a peep from his other sisters and Gerhard, who all seemed to be gazing toward the mountains. Prinz had finally regained his composure. Once again he was securely tied to the back of the wagon. He trotted behind them, head held high. Thank heaven Papa held the reins. And Papa? He stared straight ahead, no expression on his face. Clenching his jaw, Chnals tried to keep his face as vacant as his father's. After all, he was a man now.

Suddenly the storm clouds split and rays of sun poured down on them. Leaning back into the layer of dark blankets behind him, Chnals breathed in the warm, fresh air. As the scent of the wet, green, grass filled his lungs, he felt his muscles let go. A slight smile played on his face as he listened to the wheels go round and round, digging into the sticky clay. Gently he removed his favorite cap, closed his eyes, and let the sun warm his face.

He sighed a giant sigh of relief. At least they were all safe. For now. But would the people in Kasi Jurt...? He shuddered and willed his mind to shut off his fears. They had all survived. That's what really mattered. He had to trust that Oma and Opa and his friends had escaped, and they would all meet again soon. Besides, the man who owned the mill in their village was close friends with the head of Kasi Jurt, and Ohm Franz had housed and cared for his son, Abdul, while he went to school in the German settlement.

Minutes later Chnals heard Papa cluck at the horses and he felt several jolts. What was that? He jerked up and looked around. No problem. Just wood stumps at the top of the hill. The wagon rolled over the stumps and headed down.

He could now see outlines of the village below. His mind jumped with boyhood curiosity. He had never been to Kasi Jurt. At least not when he was old enough to remember. What would the people be like? What would the boys his age be like? And how about their homes? And their food?

As they neared the village, he could clearly see the houses. He stared. There were so many, many one-story houses all shoved together with no land between them. They looked as though they were all made of white-washed clay. But the roofs were almost flat! How strange. Why? Somehow he had expected the homes to look like the ones in Konstantinowka. But why should they? And how about the giant two-wheeled wagon pulled by an ox, rolling toward them across the field? He had never seen anything like this before.

Something niggled in his mind. How could they all talk to each other? He had asked Papa last night, but Papa had waved his question away. The majority of the people in Kasi Jurt spoke only Turkish, and the German people spoke mostly German. The German people had all studied Russian in school, but didn't speak the language fluently. Hopefully a few men on both sides spoke Russian well enough to understand each other, and could translate to the rest of them.

Minutes later the line of wagons rattled into a large meadow nearby, filled with grazing sheep and horses.

"Whoa!"

"Whoa!"

"Whoa!" The word rang through the meadow numerous times as the men in each wagon pulled the reins, and the wagons lurched to a stop. His younger sisters jumped up and headed for the back of the wagon.

Papa whirled around and frowned. "Quiet! Sit down," he commanded. "We must wait till we know if we are welcome."

Several feet away, men from Kasi Jurt, wearing traditional Cossack garb, stood in a line, obviously waiting for them. Each man wore leather boots, a tall dark hat made of sheepskin, and a wool coat over his pants and shirt. The sides of the coat were drawn together with a leather belt.

The man from the mill leaped out of his wagon and hurried to the chief. They embraced for a moment and thumped each other on the back. Then they talked for a while, no doubt in Russian. Finally they waved to the other wagons and all the men, including Papa, hurried down towards them, gathering in a close group.

About twenty minutes later Papa and the men scattered and strode back to their families. For the first time this day, Papa's face looked relaxed. He reached into his pocket and pulled out his watch.

"It is almost noon," he said, undoing the back of the wagon and letting the step drop. "We've been on the road for six hours. Come, children." He reached out his hand. "It's time to get out and stretch. Lunch is waiting for us."

Really? Lunch was waiting for them?

Mama looked puzzled too. "So it's okay if we stay?"

Papa nodded quickly and whispered, "Yes. Yes. They know. Some of the men rode down to check the fires and the damage."

Mama leaned forward, tears filling her voice. "What did they see? Is everything gone?"

Papa looked away. "Not now," he whispered. "Come, girls," he called out.

All the girls ran to the back of the wagon and down the step. They jumped onto the long grass and dashed about with several other children from the wagons near them. Gerhard slipped down and slumped against the wagon near Prinz.

Mama gently picked up little Maria from the blankets next to Chnals and handed her to him. Papa put out his hand for

Mama. As she stepped down from the wagon, Chnals noticed again how much her tummy had grown. He wanted to ask when the new baby was due, but he dared not. It was one of those things no one in his family discussed with the children.

He climbed out and followed Papa, with Gerhard right behind him. They joined the other men standing at the head of the group with the Muslim men, then headed into the village. The women and girls hurried close behind. The youngest children dashed around the meadow, some poking each other, screaming, laughing, and skipping.

When they neared the houses, Chnals noticed many women huddled together on the side of the village, heads bent, their arms folded in front of them. They wore long dark dresses over wide pants and leather high-top shoes. Dark headscarves were wrapped loosely around their heads, covering their hair. Only their faces showed. He tried not to stare. As they passed the group of women he saw several of them quietly wiping tears from their cheeks.

"Papa," he whispered. "Are they okay?"

Papa nodded. "They know what happened to us."

"Oh." he said. Somehow he had thought they wouldn't care or understand. After all, they were so different.

Slowly the Muslim women joined some of the German ones and nodded to them. The German women nodded back. Then the Muslim women beckoned to them to follow. He saw them disappear into several houses. *What now?*

A few minutes later, Mama appeared at one of the doors. She bowed her head to the Muslim woman next to her, then headed toward Papa. Quietly Chnals slid up next to Papa to listen.

Papa put his arm around Mama. "Are you okay?"

Mama wiped tears and blew her nose. "They're so kind." She pointed to the woman at the house nearby. "They're giving our family their best bedroom." She nudged her growing tummy. "She noticed."

Chnals turned as he heard the head of the village call out in Russian from the steps of a small mosque nearby. "Come, come. Dinner is waiting."

STORY 7
Kasi Jurt

ANNA

"**T**IME FOR A *coffee break, everyone,*" *Grandpa said as he stood up from his old wooden kitchen chair and headed to one of the tables.*
Aunt Jessie grabbed a dish of peanut butter cookies off the table and called out as she handed them to my youngest cousins. "Who wants to come and help me feed the chickens?" *Moments later she hurried out of the shed towards the chicken barn. The children dashed after her, munching cookies and squabbling about who would get the honor of carrying the buckets of grain and water. By this time I was fourteen and did not consider myself one of the "kids."*
All the rest of us got up and stretched. Aunt Anne, always the auntie who could make us all laugh, hurried to the table, doing a little dance. "Boy, I don't remember anything about Kasi Jurt!"
Aunt Helen shook her head and frowned as she hurried after her and poured coffee and hot water for tea into several mugs. She harrumphed at Aunt Anne and nudged her. "Of course not! That was at least a month before you were born!"
The rest of the aunties and uncles roared with laughter and even

my sister Lee, the two cousins my age, and I snickered as we rushed to the table to get some cookies and chocolate milk.

Everyone gathered around again and continued to talk. The men chatted about how large a crop of wheat they expected this fall, and how blessed they all were to live in a country like Canada. The women shared the patterns they were using to create quilts for the homeless people in Winnipeg.

But Grandpa stood by himself and gazed out to the east, into the vast distance of the miles of flat prairie. Smoke rose in the far area over the Sandy Lands Forest Reserve. Another forest fire, so common in August.

About fifteen minutes later, we gathered again and sat down in our chairs. With a catch in his voice, Grandpa said, "We must never forget the people in Kasi Jurt. How they welcomed us, fed us, and gave us a place to stay." He turned to us grandkids. "You all need to remember the stories of how these people protected us and saved us from the bandits."

Aunt Helen looked down toward the dirt floor, her frame bent, and folded her hands. I saw them tremble on her lap. "I was only fifteen." She swallowed hard. "I was so sure we would all die that day. I wish Mama was still alive . . . ." Her voice trembled. At last she said, "She's the person who should tell these stories. She got so close to some of the women there, even though they didn't speak the same language. They even taught each other to bake their different kinds of bread."

Grandpa lowered his head and stared at the pictures the aunties had placed on the table with the coffee and cookies. His cheeks quivered, but he said nothing.

I glanced at the pictures of the family still in Russia, and then one taken shortly after they'd arrived in Manitoba. My grandmother had been forty-four years of age at the time and she died in her fifties. Why so young, I wondered? Oh, my gosh! Of course. She *had turned from a young, dark haired woman to an old woman with gray hair, all within in a couple of years. And suddenly I felt the pain she must have felt to birth the youngest two, and guide and nurture nine children through those years of terror, famine, running, and hiding, fearing for their lives. I gulped.*

"You know, children." Dad turned to my cousins, my sister, and me. "I was only twelve, but I will never forget what it was like to come to that village and be greeted like family by people so different. We didn't even know them. I sometimes think about it and I wonder if we would have been that gracious and kind."

I held my breath for a second. Wow, he had been two years younger than I was now! How could he have survived what he was forced to do at the time?

I remembered how often my mom and dad helped people in the community who had so much less than we did. Like the checks Dad sent out every month that he and Mom never talked about when we were around. And a few months ago, when Mom gave my best dress to a girl whose family was poor, because she had no special dress for her graduation. I was mad at the time.

Now I finally understood.

CHNALS

The Meadow in Kasi Jurt.

Chnals turned as he heard the head of the village call out again in Russian from the steps of the small mosque nearby. "Come, come. The food is waiting."

They headed to the center of the village, a square covered with clay bricks. A few beech trees lined one side. Women hurried out from different households carrying plates and several pots with ladles. They placed them on a high table in the middle of the square.

"Time to eat," the head of the village called out.

Chnals felt his stomach rumble. Yes, it was time to eat. But what would the food be like? Would he like it? Well, he would pretend, smile, and nod like Papa and Mama had taught all of them to do so as not to hurt people's feelings.

He glanced around. No tables or chairs. Where would they sit? Then he noticed the Muslim men grab a plate, fill it with food, and sit down on the ground, legs crossed. They motioned for the German people to follow. Obviously confused, several young people milled about for a while, not seeming to know what to do next. The miller, Mr. Tabert, nodded, headed to the table, and helped himself. Holding their children's hands, the rest of the villagers followed.

When it was finally Chnals's turn, he examined each pot of food carefully. One plate was filled to overflowing with flat bread. That should be good. He took a piece. Next to it stood a big pot full of boiled pieces of lamb. No problem. Then a pot of beans. Then a pot of square flaps that looked like noodles boiled in some kind of broth. It reminded him of *spetzel*. He took a little and poured some strange-looking sauce over it, as he had seen his parents do.

Minutes later, they all gathered in family groups, sat down on the ground, and closed their eyes. Each family said their prayer of thanksgiving, then dug into the food, in complete silence.

"*Sehr gut*! Very good!" Katerina smacked her lips.

The others all grabbed some flatbread, dipped it in beans, and gobbled it down.

That night the entire family, still fully dressed, piled their blankets onto the decorative handmade rug on the dirt floor of the bedroom. Chnals lay awake, listening to Papa snore and Mama groan a bit. The others, except Helena, had fallen fast asleep almost immediately. Every time Chnals dipped into slumber, he jolted awake with vivid dreams of the world on fire, and dangerous men on horses chasing him down the trail with gunfire exploding in his ears.

The next morning was Sunday, and the family collected outside to eat their own breakfast of bread, cheese, and jam. Then several of the villagers gathered together in the meadow to talk and check on the children at play. Chnals sat alone for a while and looked around.

Mount Elbrus. He took in a deep breath. It was still there. The same. So peaceful. So big. So steady.

He turned to watch several young Muslim children run up to play tag with the children from their village. Except for a few, none of them seemed to have a worry about the world or each other. Even at the age of only twelve, Chnals watched and shook his head. *How amazing young children were!* Suddenly he felt old.

He noticed the teenage boys standing huddled together with the men and decided to join them. Maybe they would know what had happened to the German villages. Could they go home soon? Could they all start over again? As the German population grew in Russia, they had bought all that land to explore, expand, and make a good living. So why not now? The fires couldn't have done that much damage!

Just then he saw four riders on horses gallop over the hill toward the meadow. Chnals gulped and held his breath. Were the Tatars coming to rob and kill them? He checked to make sure no other horses ran up behind them. Only four. They wore clothes like people from the German villages. He breathed again and watched.

They leaped off their horses and hurried to a small cluster of men gathered around the minister. Oh, no! He could tell by the way their faces scrunched up and the speed with which they sprinted from their horses, not even waiting for them to stop, that the news was bad. Something had happened. But what? Loud murmurs rumbled through the crowd. Chnals's heart pounded so hard, he wanted to run and run and run. He didn't want to know . . . but at the same time, he did! He had to find out!

He hurried to the men just in time to see the minister step away from the small group and drag himself up onto one of the wagons. Mr. Toews stood tall, his face drawn and white, his voice tense. "Today is Sunday. We gather here for church at ten a.m. Make sure you all come."

At ten a.m. the German villagers gathered, sitting on cans and boxes in the meadow. Mr. Toews stepped to the front and stood at a tall wooden box from one of the wagons. He placed his Martin Luther Bible on it, opened it and thumbed to a page, then stopped. One of the men played his flute and the congregation, head bowed, sang a favorite German hymn.

Mr. Toews cleared his throat and said, "Let us read Psalm 121. 'I will lift up mine eyes unto the hills, from whence cometh my help.'" Lifting his head, he gazed out toward the Caucasus Mountains. "'My help cometh from the Lord which made heaven and earth. . . .'" His voice rose as he read the rest of the chapter. "'The Lord shall preserve thy going out and thy coming in from this time forth, and even for evermore.'" He looked into the eyes of his congregation. "This far the Lord has led us." His voice cracked. "We have news about our villages. This morning we sent four of our young men back to check."

The men stumbled to the front, faces bleak. The oldest of the men stepped forward and said, "It's all gone. They've stolen and burned everything. Even the cattle, the horses, and the chickens are gone or lying dead on the streets."

Chnals heard gasps all around him, and the wails of the people rose to the point of drowning out the words. Some wilted to the ground. All gone. And what about Oma and Opa? Suddenly he felt an anger rise to the surface he had never felt before. He wanted to scream, to kill those men, shoot them down. But he knew the old men would say that it was not their way, and they were in charge. God had commanded them not to kill . . . to love their enemy.

And what had happened to that loving God that had promised to protect them? Missing! He had betrayed them! Could Chnals ever trust Him again? They had done nothing wrong and yet they were being punished.

At the end of the service the minister said, "It's time to go back to Ukraine. Back to the villages we came from seventeen years ago. We'll be safe there."

"What?" One of the young men jumped up and shouted. "That's a twelve-hundred *werst* trip! We are thirty families! And what about the poor and sick among us? They'll never survive the journey."

Mr. Toews picked up his hat from the grass and handed it to one of the men nearby. "We will vote to form a committee to help us plan. Please pass this around." His voice was firm. "It's time to step up and live what Jesus taught us. Give as much as you can to help those who have a great deal less than you do. Together we'll survive."

STORY 8

Where now?

ANNA

GRANDPA STRODE TO *the table and gently picked up his 1892 Martin Luther Bible. His voice shook as he said, "Going through those days was very, very hard, but we learned so much . . . so much." He faltered for a moment and gazed out across the prairie. At last he said in a husky voice, "More than anything, what we learned in those years is that we are all God's children. And we all deserve kindness, help, and love. It doesn't matter what color, country, religion, or culture people come from. We're all here together. No one ever knows when they will come on hard times like we did, so children, remember you are the lucky ones, and always treat those in need with kindness and love."*

Dad nodded.

Grandpa grabbed a cup of coffee and sat down near Aunt Helena. "Chnals and Helena, why don't you tell everyone what it was like to get to know the people in Kasi Jurt?"

CHNALS

Two weeks in Kasi Jurt

The morning after their church meeting in the meadow in Kasi Jurt, Chnals got up even before the sun rose and straightened his long-sleeved, dark shirt. He had again slept very little. Stroking back his short cropped brown hair, he checked the others to make sure they were still asleep. The whole family except Papa slept peacefully in their blankets on the dirt floor.

He stepped outside the house and watched as the four young men from their village, armed with rifles, galloped into the meadow with the goats, just like they had the day before. He ran to hear the news. The sentinels jumped off their horses and rushed to the village, yelling, "The bandits are coming. The bandits are coming. Hurry! We need to hide."

Papa rushed toward the house. Panicked, Chnals ran after him. "What can we do Papa?" Papa pushed him into the house. "It's all decided. The men spoke of a plan last night. Blankets. We need blankets."

As arranged, all the German people fled into the houses and the men flung blankets over the women and children to hide them and keep them quiet. Then the men sat near a window where they could communicate with the Muslim men who were helping them, Several Muslim men stood guard in the village square with guns strung over their shoulders. They waited, and waited. But no one came. According to the village men, the bandits had stopped momentarily and then sped away.

Chnals took a deep, deep, breath and almost collapsed. Maybe the bandits still had not discovered where they were hiding. He walked toward the center of the meadow and looked around until he could see Mount Elbrus. Yes, it was still there just as always, so faithful, so steady. They were safe.

That afternoon Papa whispered to Mama and rose from the box chairs and table the men had created for the families. He strode toward the meadow. Chnals dashed after him. He knew what they were going to discuss: their escape route to Ukraine and other German villages in Russia. Their family would no doubt attempt to flee to his father's parents place in Bakhmut, Ukraine. According to his father his parents had lots of land and would need their help. He had never met his grandparents, Ungers. How strange. He imagined his grandparents would have plenty of room for all of them, and they would build a new home for the family on all that land. He drew in his breath. Home! What was that? He could barely remember.

In the blink of an eye, his mind rushed back to home. He shivered. Oh no! Where were Oma and Opa Schmidt? Were they alive? Would he ever see them again?

No! He couldn't think that way. At last he stood up straight and called out to Papa. "Can I come?"

Papa shook his head and kept on walking. "You're too young. You know that only the head of each household can come and vote. You stay and look after your mother and sisters."

Chnals wheeled around, clenched his jaw, and stomped back to the village center. Always the same. Old enough to take care of his siblings and mother, but not old enough to help make decisions and vote!

That night there was still no news of when they would leave. He tried to listen to the whispering of Mama and Papa before they rolled into their blankets. But he could make out only snatches of words that made no sense.

A day later, Chnals gathered with some of the young men who had snuck into the meeting. As soon as they neared the older men, the men stopped talking and stood back staring at them. No one said a word about the group decision, but each night more and more German families disappeared. What was happening?

Chnals tugged at Papa's arm. "What's going on?"

Papa frowned. "We have to get out of here. We're not safe."

Chnals swallowed hard. "Are the Tatars coming?"

Papa straightened and kept frowning, but said nothing.

Chnals felt his whole body tremble again. "Where have the families gone?" he insisted.

At last Papa turned to him. "Shhh. Don't tell the others. They are leaving to go to the train station. In Chassow Jurt. We can't all go together or the bandits will find us."

Chnals drew in his breath and swallowed hard. Chassow Jurt was forty *werst* away. "When are WE leaving?" he said.

Papa shrugged. "I don't know. But Chnals, you children have to stay close to the village in case we need to leave in a hurry!" Papa said in a stern voice.

Every day Chnals watched and waited. And waited. Papa and Mama said nothing about when the family would leave. Chnals missed his home, his friends, his old life. But each day turned to night, then morning again.

One day as he neared the village center, he could see a few of the elderly German men and some younger Muslim men stacking bricks in a square on top of each other. How strange. Why? He stopped near one of the beech trees, sat down on the long grass, and watched. When they were finished, they placed a piece of lead on top of the bricks and one on the front side.

Mama hurried out of the house and brushed past him with a large metal bowl of flour and a bottle of yeast.

Curious, he ran after Mama and touched her shoulder. "What's going on?" He pointed at the stack of bricks.

Mama smiled and handed the bowl to him. "Come see. That's our new oven. We need to bake bread, but we can't use the village stoves."

"Why not?" Chnals snatched the bowl from Mama and followed her to the table in the center of the square.

She smiled again. It was nice to see his mother smile. "The women here don't bake their bread in a closed oven like we do."

Strange. "Really?" He placed the metal bowl next to the others on the table.

"Yes. They do things differently than we do. They just use the top grate to cook their food. No baking. They make flat bread, you know. So their stoves don't need to be closed up like an oven."

Oh, of course. He had eaten some of their flat bread made of rice flour, but somehow he hadn't realized it had been toasted, not baked. He hurried over to the brick "thing" and examined it. He could see it now. It could double for an oven.

Moments later, more German women strode to the table and placed their bowls filled with flour next to Mama's bowl. Several Muslim women, whispering excitedly with each other, began to gather behind them. They leaned their heads toward the table, hands folded in front. One of the women, tossing back her bright green head-covering, placed a wooden bucket of steaming water with a ladle on the table.

Soon all the Muslim women were chattering, exclaiming, and pointing as the German women placed the yeast and water into the flour, and kneaded the bread, over and over again. The women gasped as they saw the bread rise. Mama placed the loaves into the makeshift oven, and Chnals took a deep breath and his mouth began to water at the familiar smell. He closed his eyes for a moment and returned to home. How often the smell of homemade bread had greeted him after school! If only he could turn back time.

When the loaves were finally baked, all the women gathered around the table. The German women cut the bread with their giant knives and slathered it with butter. Then they handed it out to their new friends, and then to the German people now gathered around them. Chnals watched, wide eyed. He would never forget that look of absolute pleasure as they all munched on the warm bread.

Mama stood back and said, "Tomorrow they have promised to show us how they make their flat bread. Chnals, you and Helena should come and watch, just in case you need to know how to do this sometime."

He nodded. He knew what she meant. Just in case they had no yeast or good people to build ovens for them on their nearly thousand-mile escape to Ukraine.

STORY 9
Left Behind

ANNA

G RANDPA TURNED TOWARD *my dad. "I think, Chnals, you have a story you want to tell the children."*
Dad nodded, looked down, then straightened, and got up from his oak kitchen chair. I could see his jaw clench as he walked toward the center of the group. He stopped near me, hesitated, then turned to face my cousins, my sister, and me.
Clasping his hands in front of his heart, he took a deep, deep breath and exhaled with a sigh, as though he was trying to release all the pain he had felt in his youth, and finally cleanse himself. My heart began to beat with his, and tears filled my eyes. I knew the story he was about to tell us. He had told it to me several times. And even as a young child it had stuck deep in my heart.

CHNALS

Each day Chnals stood at the beech tree in the square and watched the children sing and play games. Several Muslim boys his age laughed, ran, tumbled over each other, as they hit a large ball with their hands. Chnals slumped onto the crisp brown leaves on the ground and covered his face. How he missed playing, swimming, laughing with his friends! Now they were gone. Would he ever see them again? Had the families made it to the train station?

He was twelve years old. He should be out playing games, having fun, and jumping into the Caspian Sea, not hiding in a house, covered by blankets, waiting to be attacked by bandits. It wasn't fair.

Then, a few days later, one of the Muslim boys, obviously the leader of the group, dashed by him and smiled. He stopped and called out something Chnals couldn't understand. The boy beckoned to him with his head and muscled arm. He could almost hear the boy say, "Come on!" In an instant Chnals felt his heart leap in his chest and run with the boys. But, would Papa be mad if he joined them and left the village? He didn't care. He needed some fun, some way to stop feeling this deep sadness. Smiling, he nodded back, and dashed into the group.

It had been two weeks now since Chnals and his family had left home, and they were still in Kasi Jurt, still housed by the people there. Only a few German families remained. The villagers here seemed to want them to stay as long as possible. They had even found one of Papa's cows wandering about near the villages and had returned it to him, so the family now had lots of milk and cottage cheese.

This day, he sprinted through the village into the meadow with several Muslim boys in his new group. For the first time in weeks, he felt free. Free. Free as those white swans diving and wheeling overhead. He raised his head to the blue sky and laughed out loud.

Together they rushed to the orchard near the meadow, carrying wooden barrels. The boys plunked them under the apple trees and picked up the fallen apples. Two of his new friends scrambled up the trunks and tossed down the remaining large apples as fast as they could pick them off the nearly barren branches. The others grabbed the apples and pitched them into the barrels. Some missed and hit two of the boys and the "leader" on their backs. Chnals gasped. Would they get mad?

But the "leader" laughed and flung an apple into the middle of the group. Back and forth. Back and forth. The boys screamed and laughed as apples, like balls, flew through the air. So this was how you could communicate without words, he thought. Amazing! He couldn't understand a word they said, but he watched the faces of the boys and their actions, and he knew immediately what they felt! They all laughed and shoved one another, throwing apples at each other. It was the first time he had played since that night at home when he heard the Tatars were coming down the mountains toward them.

By noon they returned home with apples, apples, and more apples. After they dumped them on some dark wool blankets in the town square, all the boys, including Chnals, raced off with their barrels to the Sulak River to get water for the families, as they did each day. Chnals had asked Papa why they had no wells like the German villages had.

"I don't know," Papa said. "Maybe they don't have the machines to dig the wells. Or maybe all the wells they dug sprayed gas and oil, like some of our wells did."

"Oh." Of course. That could be the reason. He wished he could ask his new friends about their lives, but all he could do was guess.

They screamed as they jumped into the river and splashed each other with cold, clear water. While they dove, the boys grabbed whitefish, and then came up and dumped them squirming into the barrels of water. At last, the boy he called "Leiter" (Leader) glanced up and pointed to the disappearing sun. Leiter called out something Chnals could not understand, but then looked directly at Chnals and waved his arms toward the village.

Chnals would miss his new friends when it was his family's turn to leave Kasi Jurt. There was so much he wanted to know. If only he could speak their language.

As the group of boys struggled into the village with their barrels of water and fish, Chnals noticed an eerie quiet echo through the darkening sky. The village square was empty. None of the German people who usually gathered at the fire-pit to talk were present.

Oh, no! What had happened? He checked around. All he could see were the few Muslim men who stood watch each night with their rifles drawn. Except tonight there were more men from Kasi Jurt! More guns!

Chnals rushed to the house and dropped his bucket at the front door. The water sloshed over the edge and soaked his shoes and socks. Head bent, the mother of the house sat at the doorway, her dark shawl covering her head. She clung to her two young children, rocking them back and forth, tears running down her cheeks. Slowly, she looked up at Chnals and shook her head.

Chnals gasped and his throat turned into a knot. He dashed into the house screaming, "Papa! Mama! Papa! Mama! Where are you?"

Nothing.

Were they all covered with blankets again? Hiding? Had the Tatars found them? He dashed into the bedroom. All the blankets and clothes were gone. His knees buckled and he fell to the floor. As he covered his face with his hands, he lifted his head and screamed, "Papa! Mama!"

Nothing. They were gone

STORY 10
Rescue

ANNA

MY FATHER'S VOICE *wavered and his hands began to shake. Suddenly he whirled around and strode away. I saw him pull his white handkerchief with the embroidered C on it from his suit-jacket pocket. He shook it open and blew his nose once, then twice, and kept walking.*

I heard my cousins gasp. Moments later, five- year-old Bert dashed after my dad and tugged on his suit tails. "Uncle Chnals! Uncle Chnals!" he called out in a panicked voice. "What happened?"

My father stopped. He hesitated and I could see his chest heave as he took a deep breath. Then slowly he straightened his back, cleared his throat, and turned toward Bert. In a half kidding, half sarcastic voice dad said, "Well, I'm still here, aren't I?"

Bert cowered and bent his head as though he had been slapped.

I glanced at my mom. Her lips tight and her brows wrinkled, she hung onto the sides of her chair with both hands. I sucked in my breath and my body began to tremble. Poor Mom. We both knew what could happen next. My father needed to wail, scream, and cry, like I sometimes heard him at home in the middle of the night. Often

I heard my mother whisper when Dad started telling stories about Russia, "Chnals! Don't think about that! It just makes it worse."

I checked the rest of the family. My Aunties, frozen in place, took a deep breath and tried to smile. The cousins tittered a bit at Dad's joke, but my grandfather, face drawn, stared back into the prairie and murmured, "I'm sorry, Chnals . . . I'm so sorry."

My eyes swam in deep salty swamps and my heart sprang open and overflowed like a new spring as I watched my father cope with his deepest well of trauma the only way he knew how. Deny. Deny. Deny. Don't show your feelings. Be strong. Be strong. Be strong!

I could only imagine what it had been like for him at age twelve, believing he would never see his family again. Deserted. He was all alone in a culture, a religion, a language, a people he knew nothing about. For the rest of his life!

That's when I forgave my dad for all the eggshells I walked on for so many years, days, hours. For the many years of anger lashed out onto me when I had no idea what I had done wrong.

I finally understood.

Quickly my dad grabbed Bert's hand and led him back to the group. He paused at the table and Aunt Helen poured him another cup of coffee with cream. He took several sips, then walked toward us and stopped in front of me.

His face turned serious and he said in a strong voice, "Children. Many things happened in those six years we were running for our lives, but this is the one I remember most."

CHNALS

Wide eyed, Chnals huddled under a small, dark, wool blanket on the dirt floor in the bedroom. The night was half-gone but he had not slept. Not even a wink. Wolves bayed in the darkness. Else all was silent. Only the smell of Mama's rose-water that still hung in the air comforted him.

Nothing else remained. Even his blanket and extra clothes were gone. Had his parents forgotten him? Or had they just fled in terror when the bandits came? What if he had to live here for the rest of his life and never see his family or friends again?

Oh, why had he run out to play with those boys? Bad things happened when you were happy. He had to be strong. He could hear his father yelling in the back of his mind, "Be serious, Chnals." He closed his eyes and made a promise to himself. He would never laugh and play again.

Slowly he folded back his blanket. Barefoot, he tiptoed to the front door. It was open. He could see only a few stars sparkling between the clouds in the darkness. The man of the house sat on the brick stoop with his rifle clutched in his hand. He frowned, said something in a stern voice, then pointed one hand back to the bedroom.

Shaking, Chnals dashed back into the bedroom and fell to his knees. "Oh please, please God help me," he whispered. Silent tears spilled down his cheeks onto his muddy white, shirt. He lay down again and covered himself. At last he fell into a fitful sleep. Monstrous men slashing through the forest with guns blazing tore through his nightmares.

Suddenly he heard the whinny of a horse in the background of his nightmare.

He gasped and woke with a start. The horse whinnied again. A miracle? Prinz! He thought he heard his father's voice call,

"Whoa." Heart pounding, he sat up straight. Silence . . . and more silence. Had it all been part of the nightmare? He slumped back under the blanket.

Minutes later he heard voices and unfamiliar footsteps. The wooden door to the house creaked and the blanket hanging in front of the bedroom door, stirred. There in his room stood a man all dressed in black. He cowered under the blanket. No! The bandits! They had found him.

Chnals tried to scream, but only a tiny noise squeaked out of his throat.

The man bent down over him and murmured into his ear, "*Shh . . . shh.*"

It was Papa! Chnals covered his face with his hands and his heart felt as though it would explode with joy. Papa. He had come for him.

"Come. Now," Papa whispered. He grabbed Chnals's hand and lifted him from the floor. As he felt the damp warmth of his father's hand, he knew that he was safe. He finally understood what Mama meant when she used to say that her heart sang sweet songs of thanksgiving whenever good things happened to them.

As they tiptoed out of the house, Papa bowed a little to the men who stood near the door, holding Prinz by the reins. "*Bal'shoye spasiba.* Thank you so very much. We will never forget you," Papa said in Russian.

One of the men bowed back and touched Papa on the arm. "Are you all safe?"

"Yes, for now," Papa said as he hoisted Chnals onto Prinz's bare back and jumped up in front of him. Prinz stood motionless, as though knowing the seriousness of the situation. With barely a sound, Papa slapped the reins and they raced into the blackness.

Chnals grasped the back of Papa's fur jacket and hung on as Prinz dashed forward. For a minute he closed his eyes to help him concentrate on remaining stable and not getting too scared, but he could feel the branches of the barren trees brush past his arms, and smell the sweet scent of the pine. He noticed Papa's arm jolt back as he pulled the reins. Then he loosened his grasp and Prinz took off like lightning.

Several minutes later Papa yelled, "Whoa," and Prinz jerked to a stop in the dark forest. Chnals leaned back and let go of Papa. Where were they?

Following his father, Chnals jumped off onto the dead grass next to a muddy clay path, and peered into the blackness. Where was everybody? Were they alone? Suddenly Chnals heard a woman's whispery voice behind them.

"Chnals! Chnals!" He turned. A woman stood in the distance in the shadows of the trees.

Chnals gasped! Could it be? "Mama?" he yelled in a hoarse whisper. The woman rushed forward in her dark skirt, her black shawl loosely wound over her head and shoulders.

"Come, Chnals. Your mother is waiting." Papa pulled Chnals toward the woman.

Mama threw her arms around him and sank to the ground. Still trying to be strong, as he knew all young German men were supposed to be, he sucked in his breath and tried to stand tall.

Then she burst into tears. He felt her shake as she pulled him close. Suddenly he let go and fell into her arms."Mama, Mama," he cried.

STORY 11
Kostek

ANNA

ALL THE COUSINS *stared at Dad, mouths open, as he sat down on his kitchen chair, facing us. I could see him tremble as he folded his hands in his lap. My mother glanced at my sister and me with an expression so sad, I wanted to cry.*

Finally Dad asked, "Any questions?"

No one muttered a murmur, never mind a word. The aunties all sat still, looking down at their hands, clenched in their laps. Uncle George closed his eyes tight, and Grandpa looked into the distance again. I wished my grandma, who had died ten years after their arrival in Canada, was still alive so she could experience this moment in person. But then, maybe she was here, looking down on us all from heaven.

Finally my twelve-year-old cousin, Marie, always the "life of the party" as we used to say, raised her hand the way we had been taught in our small country school.

"Yes, Marie," my dad said. "What would you like to know?"

She hesitated. Then her questions tumbled out of her mouth as though they would never end. "What happened then? Where were you? Was everyone okay? Where were the aunties and Uncle George?" She glanced over at my aunties sitting next to the table.

My father smiled. "That is a lot of questions! But I'll try to answer them all."

Aunt Jessie stood up at the table and dumped some ice water into a large glass. She handed it to him. "Here, Chnals, You'll need this," she said softly.

He nodded and cleared his throat. "All the German people still left in Kasi Jurt on that day ran for their lives when the bandits came. They scattered and hid in the forest a few miles away. They were all very scared, but otherwise okay." He bowed a little to Grandpa. "Thank you, Papa, for coming back for me."

Grandpa nodded, looked into my dad's eyes, and added with pride in his voice, "It was Prinz who saved you! He knew where to go, even in the middle of the night with no moon. Without him we could not have found you, Chnals, and brought you back to us."

CHNALS

It had been two days since Chnals had arrived with Papa and Prinz. All the people huddled in the forest on the hillsides, everyone dressed in black garb, hushed and silent. Each evening the men gathered and waited for the sentries to return. Each day they galloped back, glum-faced, shaking their heads.

These were the words Chnals heard over and over again from Papa and all the adults around them, "*Shh . . . shh.* Someone will hear us."

Each morning, breakfast consisted of bread and cold milk. And then for lunch, bread and cold milk. And for dinner, more bread and cold milk. Thank goodness the men from Kasi Jurt had given Papa one of his cows they found wandering near the village and Papa had taken it with them when they fled.

As usual, this morning the whole family gathered around the wagon, starving and waiting for food.

"Mama, why can't we have eggs?" Sara grumbled "We have a boxful we got in Kasi Jurt!"

Mama shook her head. "*Shh*. No. You don't want a *raw* egg do you? We can't boil them."

Five-year-old Katchen jumped off the back of the wagon and scowled at Mama. "But why not? I hate bread and milk!"

Mama covered Katchen's mouth. "Quiet. Quiet. We can't build a fire. The bandits will see the smoke and smell it. They'll come after us."

Sara, obviously trying to help, ran forward, grabbed Katchen, and swung her around. "Let's play," she whispered. "But we have to be quiet." Moments later Katchen dashed through the trees with her sisters chasing her. And then it happened.

They screamed with laughter and Papa tore after them. "No! You can't play! The Tatars will hear you. You will put us all in danger!"

Chnals shook his head. "Just like girls," he muttered to himself, as he went to help Mama put out the plate of bread on a large stump nearby.

Just then he heard horses' hooves on the dank clay path nearby. The three young sentries galloped into the area, heads held high, laughing. Men from all directions ran to greet them, then gathered to talk.

Chnals held his breath and studied the group. Maybe, just maybe . . . .

Minutes later the men strode to their families, and Chnals heard a cheer rise through the forest so loud, it would have deafened any of the wolves he had heard last night.

All the children gathered in an open area nearby and ran through the trees, whooping and yelling, throwing wet leaves into the air.

Papa stopped next to Mama, the muscles in his face relaxed for the first time since Chnals had arrived in the forest. "God has answered our prayers. We are safe. We are moving on to Kostek. They say we can stay there till we can go on to Chassow Jurt. And then the train to Ukraine and my mother and father!"

Chnals let out a deep breath and closed his eyes. They would be at Grandma and Grandpa's soon.

Photos

Unger family 1923 in Russia
Back row: Katerina, Gerhard, Chnals, Helena, Sara
Front row: Justina, Mama, Elizabetha, Papa, Anna, Maria

Anna Unger Goodwin

Arrival in Manitoba, Canada at Aunt Katerina's home, 1924

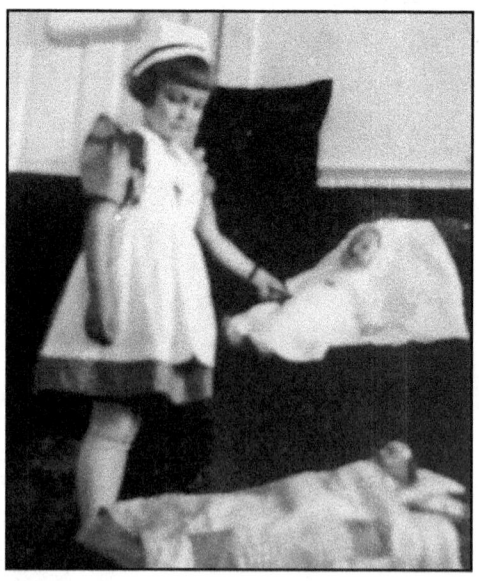

Nine-year-old Anna pretending she is a nurse

Family picture: Mother Anna, Lee, Dad Chnals
Five-year-old Anna in the front

Teenage Lee on Dad's horse Prince on the farm.

STORY 12
On the Road to Chassow Jurt

ANNA

MY TEN-YEAR-OLD COUSIN, *Dan, whipped up his hand in the air and called out to my dad, "Really? The train? I love trains! You all got to go on the train across Russia for almost a thousand miles?"*
My dad nodded and smiled. "Well, it wasn't quite that simple."
Dan turned around, facing his mother, my Aunt Maria, and said, disbelief written over his face, "Mom, you got to go too? Why didn't you ever tell us that story?"
My dad's sisters—the aunties, as we called them—burst into laughter. Aunt Maria chuckled and waved her hand from side to side. "No, no, kids. I was only two years old. I don't remember a thing. Just a little from our time in Ukraine."
Aunt Teena nudged Aunt Maria on the arm. "You remember the ship on our trip to Canada. You were eight by then."
"Oh, yes, I remember we had so much fun, even though we had to sleep on the straw with lots of other children." My dad made a face so unpleasant that I'll never forget it. As if he wanted to throw up. He had been eighteen by then, and obviously he hadn't seen that whole adventure quite the way his younger sisters had!

101

"Now let's hear what your Uncle Chnals has to say about the trip to get onto the train," my grandfather said, his voice raised as though somewhat annoyed at his grown children's outburst.

CHNALS

It had been another two long weeks now in Kostek, a Muslim village about ten miles south of Kasi Jurt, sleeping in musty wool blankets on hard clay ground. Although the women and children had been housed in the homes, there had not been room for all of the German people. Chnals had offered to sleep with the men outside in the village square. Thank God, the Tatars had not returned.

As he saw the sun crawl up higher in the partly clouded sky, Chnals, fully dressed, raised his head from his rolled-up jacket that acted as a pillow. His tummy growled. Would he ever get enough to eat again? He could feel his ribs sticking out more and more when he pulled off his shirt and jumped into the river for a cold, cold bath. He shivered thinking about it, and remembered his dirty pants dripping with muck.

The villagers generously fed them as much as they could, but the people here were poor, and each day they ate flat bread and a small dish of lamb. And of course Papa still milked his cow, although the amount of milk had dramatically decreased. Most days their cow, Mädchen, obviously stressed, stood in the green meadow with the sheep, bellowing and crying for her friends and home.

Chnals closed his eyes and covered his face with his cold, clammy hands.

Would it ever end?

Just then he heard Papa's voice. "Chnals!" Papa called out. "Chnals! It's time. Get up now! Come help. We are going to Chassow Jurt."

Chnals leaped up, his heart soaring higher than the eagle he had watched rise overhead that morning. "Papa, I'm coming! I'm coming!" He raced toward his dad. In a moment he stopped. Oh, no, he had forgotten his "bed." He turned and darted back to get his blanket and jacket. Rolling the blanket up in a bundle, he hoisted it up on his shoulder and ran toward the wagons in the meadow. Several of the German men swept mud from the beds of the wagons, loaded them with boxes filled with food, dirty clothes, and blankets. A few wild pigs rooted around the campsite, obviously looking for leftovers.

Two hours later, Papa yelled, "Okay, everyone on board. Now!" All Chnals's sisters and his brother jumped onto the wagon and took their usual places, sitting on boxes covered with dank blankets that smelled of wet wool.

Chnals turned and saw Mama struggle, then stumble, as she tried to lift her bulging body onto the back of the four-wheeled wagon. He shouted, "Mama! Be careful!"

Papa wheeled around, and Chnals could hear him gasp. He rushed to steady her. As he grabbed her under her arms, he hoisted her up. She staggered to her box and sat down, her long, damp hair tumbling around her shoulders.

Both Mama and Papa's faces were white, but they said nothing. Chnals shook his head. How long would it be until Mama had the baby? And how could they take care of an infant while they were running and hiding?

Papa jumped up onto the front of the wagon and grabbed the reins. Chnals took his usual position next to Papa in case he needed help. The bandits had left and not returned . . . but just in case. Once again, he heard Papa's voice in his head. *Chnals, you are the oldest son. You have to be strong. If anything happens to me, you take my place.*

Slowly the line of wagons rolled out of Kostek onto the swampy trails and through the bushes and forest toward Chassow Jurt, about twenty-five miles south and west. Several of the Muslim men from the village, on horseback, surrounded the wagons and galloped back and forth, their rifles tucked into their dark, homemade blanket saddles.

Surprised, Chnals leaned toward Papa and said, "What are those men doing? I thought the Tatars were gone."

Papa whispered back, "*Shh.* The children don't need to know. We have hired the men to guard us in case the mountain bandits come back." Chnals nodded and felt his muscles let go. He slumped forward. The young men from Kostek would keep them safe.

The *clack, clack* of wheels, over and over again, lulled him into rest and back to his old life. He smiled as he remembered his friends, the school, laughing, jumping into the Caspian Sea, feeding the horses and cows. For the first time in weeks, he felt a bubble of joy in his heart.

Suddenly swarms of mosquitoes whirred in large circles and buzzed over and onto the horses. The horses shrieked as they raised their legs, their hooves striking the air. Chnals gasped and hung on to the side of the wagon. Papa grabbed the reins tight and hung on as the horses bolted off the trail into the marshy forest. The wagon rocked back and forth, the wheels barely touching the land.

"No!! No! Help!" Katchen screamed as several mosquitoes landed on her face. She swatted again and again with her arms, but they kept coming.

Chnals let go of the wagon and jumped up. What should he do? Had they come all this way only to die of malaria like the early settlers before them?

Mama and Helena grabbed wet blankets crumpled on the floor and swung them hard, this way and that. All the others screamed and buried their heads in their damp, wool-covered arms. Chnals grabbed two more blankets off the boxes. He and Mama tossed them over the children as they huddled together in the wagon.

The mosquitoes rose into the air again and moved on to the other wagons.

Screams! Screams! Panic. Horses racing in all directions.

And then it was over. All that was left were large, red, itchy lumps.

Tears, tears, and pain.

A half hour later the wagons rumbled back onto the trail. Mama dipped a pillowcase into the pail of cold water next to her, and dabbed the red, swollen bumps on the children's faces and hands. Two-year-old Maria lay on the floor sobbing, a wet towel covering her face.

Without warning, Papa shoved the reins into Chnals's hands. "Here. You take the reins!"

"What's wrong?" His whole body shook as he grabbed the reins. Several Muslim guards dashed past their wagon, the men leaning forward into their horses, their faces strained and stern. He gasped, and turned to see Papa rush to the back of the wagon. What now? Then he saw the Muslim guards gather behind them and gallop towards a haze-covered hill in the distance. Chnals jumped up and stared at the rise. He gulped. At least fifty men on horseback raced out of the mist toward them.

Oh, no! The mountain bandits!

Minutes later, rifles blazed in the distance! *Bang . . . boom . . . bang*!

Chnals hung onto the reins as the horses veered into the bush and the swamp.

"Get down! Get down!" Papa yelled as he shoved all the children onto the floor of the wagon and covered them with blankets. Helena ducked behind one of the boxes.

Papa rushed to the front and stood up behind Mama, sheltering her and the coming baby with his body. Still standing tall behind Mama, he grabbed the reins back from Chnals and called out, "Whoa! Whoa!" His voice sounded calm again and in command. "Whoa, whoa," he called again. Prinz whinnied behind them. Chnals fell to his knees and hung on to the side of the wagon.

Suddenly all was quiet. Only the wind in the trees whistled nearby. What happened?

Chnals stared toward the hill, but the mass of bare bushes obscured his view. All he could see was Mount Elbrus in the distance, towering above the trees. As though hearing the silence, the horses slowed, then came to a stop. Papa gave back the reins to Chnals, and jumping over the children, he hurried to the rear of the wagon, untied Prinz, and leaped onto his back.

For the first time since the gunfire, Chnals checked around for the other wagons, now scattered at a distance. Most of the horses stood still, as though waiting. The men gathered near a large, dead fir tree, obviously trying to decide what to do next. Soon after, one of the guards rode toward them and joined the men.

Chnals bent forward, trying to study the men. He was too far away to see their faces but he saw the guard waving toward the hill. His mind raced. Were they safe? Where were the bandits? Why had they stopped shooting? Were the guards okay? When would Papa come back?

He waited . . . and waited . . . and waited. Silence.

About half an hour later, he heard horses whinny, and the Muslim guards galloped down the trail toward them. No bandits. Chnals took a deep breath and released it slowly. They were still alive and the bandits were gone. How had the guards been able to defeat them? Had they shot them all?

Shortly Papa returned, sitting tall, as he rode Prinz next to the front of the wagon. In a stern voice he said, "Time to go. Chnals, you take the wagon. I'll ride Prinz."

Chnals leaned over and whispered, "Papa. What happened?"

Papa, face drawn, said nothing and rode ahead with several other men, mingling with the guards.

Another secret. How could the families expect their oldest sons to take charge when they refused to tell them anything? His jaw went hard. He slapped the reins on the horses' backs, harder than he had planned. They dashed forward into the growing line of wagons, their hooves plopping along on the wet clay trail. They would soon be in Chassow Jurt. What then?

"Whoa!" Papa yelled. Prinz and the other horses came to a quick stop at the railroad station. Five of the older men gathered and hurried into the station. Chnals refused to sit and wait in the wagon again. No way! He had to know what was going on.

"Helena, you take the reins," he commanded. "I have to go to the bathroom." He shoved them into her hand and ran behind the station to go pee. Instead of returning, he slipped into the back door of the brick station and followed the men down a corridor. He stood and watched in the shadow of a large luggage cart. At the desk, the men pulled out many rubles from their pockets and held them up to the clerk.

The clerk shook his head and said in Russian. "I can't sell you tickets. It's against the law now. The train has to stay open for the soldiers. They come often. At any time! Here," he pointed to the man beside him. "This is the conductor of our next train leaving north from Chassow Jurt."

Mr. Schultz from Village #5 strode forward, grabbed all the rubles from the others and plunked them down on the desk. "These are all for you if you help us get to Suworowka. Can you do that?"

The conductor, in his dark wool uniform, marched to the desk and picked up the money. His lips stiffened and he glared at the men. "Only if you understand that we cannot guarantee anything. No animals. If the White or the Red Army comes, we will have to throw you off wherever we are, and you will have to hide. We can't help you, or else they'll kill you and us too. Then they'll steal the train and everything you own."

The five men looked at each other and murmured in German, too low for Chnals to hear. Finally he saw the men nod.

"Come back in two days. If the army is not here, we will leave at five o'clock in the morning."

ANNA

Grandpa stood up and clapped his hands. "It's late."

All the cousins began to buzz, turning to face Grandpa and my dad.

Dan stood up and called out, "That's not fair. What happened?"

My father looked at Grandpa with a question mark plastered on his face. Grandpa finally nodded. "Okay. Uncle Chnals will answer a few questions."

Dad stroked his throat as though pushing down his words. "Yes, we left two days later. We hid in the cattle cars. But first we had to sell our wagons and our horses."

I frowned. "Did you have to sell Prinz too?"

My dad glanced at my grandfather, whose eyes were glazed and his hands clasped. He blinked several times. Head held high, he turned and stared into the distant prairie again.

Dad reached out to Grandpa and touched him on the shoulder. "Yes. We sold the wagon and horses, but your grandpa did not sell Prinz, He gave him to one of the guards, a gentle soul. So brave. He helped us all so much in Kostek and on this trip. Those men saved our lives." He glanced at my Aunt Anne. "Even Anne, who was not born yet."

I bowed my head. Poor Grandpa. There was a gentle soul inside of him too, even though he was too proud to show it to us most of the time. But it all made sense. For many years Dad had a favorite horse that he rode every day. His name , , , Prince.

Grandpa clapped again. "Children, it is time to go home and milk the cows. We'll continue the story next year on our Thanksgiving Day. Always remember. Never let your freedoms go."

The aunties got up from their chairs and picked up the coffee pot, the jug of cold water, and the cookies, and headed toward the house. Dan refused to move and raised his hand. "I don't understand. Why did the Mountain Tatars not kill you all, when they were up on that hill? What happened to them?"

Grandpa grumped at Dan. "Next time, I said!"

But next time never came. Grandpa died of cancer in May and our Thanksgiving Day gatherings in August ended.

STORY 13
On the Train to Suworowka
The Birth of a Sister

ANNA

THAT NEXT FALL, *still at the age of fourteen, I entered high school in the town several miles from our farm. I was a lucky teenager, as several of my friends frequently reminded me. My parents had the money to send me to school and board with a family in town. Most of the kids in my elementary school took correspondence classes from grades nine through twelve.*

Each Friday evening my dad drove twenty miles to bring me home for the weekend, unless our dirt-and-gravel roads became impassable. During winter storms my four aunties, who lived much closer to town, picked me up and I stayed with them on Grandpa's farm. Often I would sneak up to the attic and read their magazines, especially their copies of Ladies Home Journal. *And sometimes, while the snowstorm raged outside so loud it whistled and screamed like a train crashing into the house, I'd huddle on the sofa near the fireplace and shiver. Although they said nothing, I saw my aunties glance at each other and nod. Then they gathered close around me, and told funny stories of the early years in Russia before the revolution.*

One weekend, after the roads were cleared, my dad came to pick me up at the aunties' farm. Of course they asked us to stay for supper. I could smell the sweet odor of freshly made varenike with cream gravy, a Ukrainian dish, often served in our family. "Dad, can we stay?" I begged.

"I don't know, Anna," Dad muttered. "It's getting late. It'll be dark soon. And they're predicting another storm!"

"Come on, Chnals." Aunt Jessie said. "These are homemade. We spent a lot of time making them just for you."

My dad's face lifted into a smile. I smiled inside but kept my face flat. Of course, I knew I had won, but I didn't want Dad to see victory indelibly written on my face.

Aunt Anne rushed about covering the antique oak table with a fresh linen tablecloth. Aunt Betty set out the flowered china plates and I dashed to the cupboard. I pulled out the serviettes and the silverware and placed them in perfect British style... the forks and serviette on the left, and the knife and spoons on the right.

Before we ate, we all bowed our heads and folded our hands. In unison we said the usual German prayer to thank God and to bless the food. Then my dad added, as he so often did, "Thank you, God, for our freedom and for all the people who helped us stay safe and come to free soil." His voice cracked as he said, "And thank you, God, for Papa."

When we raised our heads, I noticed tears in all my aunties' eyes. Total silence. Normal behavior for my dad, but very unusual for the aunties, especially the younger ones. They loved to talk and laugh.

At last my Aunt Helen wiped her eyes with the napkin and said, her voice shaking, "I miss Papa. He was such a strong and wise man."

The others all nodded and began to tell stories of Grandpa.

Suddenly my brain flashed into fast drive. Oh, no! I burst out, "Grandpa said he would tell us this year what happened when Aunt Anne was born. But he's gone. Was she born on the train?"

Dad frowned at me. I took a deep breath, trying not to show my childlike fear. I was sure he'd scold me in his good German manner, like he so often had in the past. "Shh. Don't talk with your mouth full," But instead he glanced at the others, who nodded. He poured some hot coffee into his saucer and took a sip. "Not now. After dinner."

Slowly he added more varenike *and cream gravy to his plate, picked up his fork and knife, and continued eating. The aunties chattered on about their friends and the recent snowstorm, but I could tell by the way Dad stared out the frosted window that his mind was far, far away in Russia.*

CHNALS

April 23, 1918

Chnals woke with a start as the train lurched to a stop. He gasped. What had happened? He glanced out the window. The moon stared back at him with that ugly bright face. He knew by now darkness remained their best friend. But there shone the moon, threatening their safety.

The conductor in his dark uniform and hat rushed through the door of the cattle car, waving his hands. He yelled, "Wake up! Get out! Now! The Red Army is coming. They will kill us all if they find you here!"

The twenty or so people huddling together on the straw jumped to their feet and rushed toward the door. The elderly ones wavered and fell back onto the floor of the train, crying out as the younger ones pushed them forward.

"Stop! Stop!" one of the old men yelled. No one seemed to listen.

"Get out, get out. Leave nothing behind," the conductor shouted again.

Chnals heard Mama moan behind him, and he whirled around. She held on to her swollen belly and panted hard. He noticed the skirt of her dress was wet. Oh, no! The baby was coming! He knew about birth. He had seen several calves and piglets born.

Papa grabbed Mama and lifted her gently into his arms, his face tight but unyielding. He whispered, "Chnals. Grab the children. I have to take care of Mama."

Chnals gritted his teeth. Quick. He had to be strong. He had to help. Chnals nodded and turned to the others. He knew how to take charge by now. "*Shh* . . . quiet. We have to go. Grab your bags. Hold hands," he commanded. He glanced at Maria curled up on the straw, shaking, her hands covering her face. Obviously she was trying hard not to cry or make a sound. Poor girl. She didn't understand. "Helena, you carry Maria."

Quickly they filed behind each other, still grasping hands, and blended into the group. One by one they jumped down off the train. He heard the squish of his shoes as they hit wet clay.

Wilhelm, one of the young men, stopped by the conductor and said in Russian, "Where are we? Are we in Suworowka?"

The conductor shook his head but said nothing.

Glancing back, Chnals saw Papa and another man lift Mama to the ground. A young woman hovered over her as well. "Chnals," Papa called, waving his hands toward the dark forest about a hundred feet away. "Hurry! You stay together. Now run. We'll meet you there."

"Hold hands," Chnals ordered his younger siblings again. "Don't let go. See that clump of pine trees on the left? We'll wait for Papa and Mama there."

As though they were a well trained army, they rushed to obey. Other small groups ran past them for cover. In the distance he heard guns, then horses' hooves, and the bellows of men coming toward them. The soldiers!

"Hurry, hurry," he called, forgetting to remain quiet. Would Papa and Mama make it on time? What would they do if they didn't? No, no! He couldn't think about that now.

When they reached the forest they slumped down low between the trees. He breathed in the sweet scent of pine and tried to relax. Minutes later Papa appeared, holding Mama. He placed her down onto the thick green grass. She raised herself and leaned against the heavy trunk of a tree. Brushing aside her dark, sweat-drenched hair, she closed her eyes. Suddenly she buckled in half and, without a sound, mouthed pain. Chnals gasped. He had no idea having a baby was this hard!

About fifteen minutes later he heard the whistle of the train. In the moonlight, men swooped onto the railroad cars, their rifles held high. He sucked in his breath and held it. And then they were gone. He let out a giant sigh and his mind cleared. They were safe.

At least for now.

As the group wound its way on a well worn trail through the forest, wolves howled in the distance. It was clear they were not in Suworowka. But where were they? Slowly the trees began to thin, and in the full moonlight he could see an old, weathered, farmhouse and barn.

A cheer rose from the group.

"Thank goodness, we are here," Papa said as he stopped to place Mama on a tree stump. "The people here will help us."

But when they reached the house and barn, it became clear the farm was abandoned. No lights. Only a few chickens and a lone cow and her calf wandered through the front yard. The women and children huddled together near Mama, whispering to each other.

Wilhelm shoved open the front door of the house and stood back as though waiting for something to happen. Moments later, he went inside, lit a lamp and waved for the other men to follow. Chnals hurried after them. He gagged as the stench of rotting meat hit his nostrils. Dirty clothes and old food lay strewn throughout the kitchen and living room.

Wilhelm headed down the hall with the lamp and turned into the first room on the left. Chnals heard a cry and the lamp crashed to the floor. A light flared up.

"Wilhelm, Wilhelm! What's wrong?" Papa yelled. He rushed into the room. "Throw that blanket over the fire. Now!" The light flared one more time, then disappeared.

Young Peter ran into the room and screamed out, "They're dead. They're all dead! They've been shot!"

A minute later Papa came to the door, hands folded, head bowed. "God help us," he said quietly.

Shaking, Chnals hurried to Papa's side, but Papa shooed him away. "This is not for young boys." Chnals gritted his teeth. As always, Papa expected him to be strong and in charge, but only when it suited Papa. Didn't he know Chnals would be thirteen next month? "Take Mama and the others outside to the barn," Papa ordered.

Struggling not to cry, Chnals rushed to where Mama and his sisters sat. He led Mama, stumbling to the worn wooden barn, and the other kids hurried behind in silence. A few women in their group from the train followed them. And so did the moonlight. Thank you, moon, he whispered in his mind.

Helena swaddled Maria in her arms and bent her head low

over her little sister. Her tight brown braids fell over bent shoulders. As Chnals shoved open the giant barn door, he tiptoed inside and felt a squish on his already filthy boots. Oh, oh. What was that? The sudden stench of chicken, pig, and cow dung nearly overwhelmed him. He tried not to breathe in. Then he gulped and swallowed hard as he heard two of the girls behind him retch and spew liquid all over him and Mama. Thank goodness, they had eaten nothing except dried bread in the last two days.

More chickens fluttered up from the straw around them, almost hitting him in the face. A black kitten jumped into the air and yowled, then landed in the straw, and lay still, its body shaking.

For the first time, Mama smiled. "Help me get down here on that clean straw, Chnals. Near *Katzchen* ," she said. She bent over to stroke the long, straggly hair of the skinny kitten. "Chnals, you must milk that cow and give some milk to *Katzchen*."

He nodded. "Yes, Mama, I will." He checked the area and shoved away some old horse manure with his foot, then helped Mama down.

She suddenly buckled again and covered her face with her hands, groaning. Oh no. What should he do? He looked around. The woman who had paid special attention to Mama at the train stood near the door, and he ran to her, heart pounding. "Can you help my mama? Please."

She glanced at Mama and rushed past him to her side, kneeling on the straw. She felt Mama's belly. "Children, you get your father, and get me some water and boil it. Quick! And some soap. We must have clean blankets." She felt Mama's tummy again and shook her head. Chnals hurried to her side and saw something jump a little under Mama's skirt. The baby! Was it attempting to get out? "Now go! Your mother has had several babies. It won't be long," the woman said.

Chnals had no idea what all that meant, but he didn't question. Thank goodness, the woman knew about childbirth... and he knew about following orders.

"Time to go," he commanded. He gathered the others and ushered them out the barn door. "Girls, you go get Papa and see if you can find some clean blankets and soap. Gerhard and I will get the water and heat it."

"Clean blankets... and soap? Where do we find those?" Sara grumped and stomped her foot. "We have no clean blankets, Chnals. Everything is dirty! You know that."

He shrugged and shook his head. "Ask Papa. You check the house." He grabbed Gerhard and a rusty metal bucket that lay near the door of the barn, and they dashed down to the stream nearby.

The full moon now shone high in the sky, illuminating the sparkling creek as it rushed down the hill. And this time he whispered a thank-you to the moon. How strange. It could hide you with its absence, but it could also lead you to safety with its presence.

As he dipped the bucket into the roaring stream, the water rushed inside and almost swept him away. Chnals grabbed onto the bare bush next to him and hung on with one hand. He panted, as he rolled back onto the grass, the bucket wavering back and forth in his other hand.

"Chnals! Chnals!" Gerhard yelled as he raced toward Chnals. He fell to his knees and grabbed the bucket in both hands.

"It's okay. It's okay." Chnals got up, his entire body shivering from the cold water. He picked up the bucket and ran toward the house.

"How are we going to make the water hot?" Gerhard called from behind. "The woman said the water had to be boiled!"

"I know how to do it. Now keep quiet, Gerhard." Chnals had already created the perfect plan in his mind. Get the water to the house. Pour it into one of the pots he had noticed in the kitchen. One of the men would know how to light the stove. Then all he would need to do was wait until the water boiled, pour the water back into the bucket and run it to Mama.

As they turned the corner around the barn, he saw the figures of four men with shovels hurry to the house. He stopped and wheeled around, placing one hand on Gerhard's arm. "*Shh.* Wait."

They stood still and watched as the men strode into the side garden. Moments later he heard the shovels hit dirt, the men talking in low voices.

"What are they doing?" Gerhard whispered.

"I don't know," Chnals whispered back. He turned and suddenly saw large lumps in blankets lying near the front door. The bodies! His heart thumped hard against his chest. Finally he took a deep breath. He had to be strong! He turned to Gerhard. "It's nothing. Don't worry. They are our men." He attempted a smile. "Let's go to the back door so we don't disturb them."

His plan had worked.

At the barn door, Papa grabbed the handle of the bucket of hot water from Chnals. "Now go stay with your sisters and brother. I'll come out to get you when it's time." He rushed back into the barn, slamming the door behind him.

Chnals cringed. Now what? He checked around and noticed his sisters and Gerhard in their thick wool jackets, visibly shivering as they huddled in the straw beside the barn. Helena held Maria close on her lap. He could hear the breathing of his siblings. Some had obviously fallen asleep. He closed his eyes, but all he saw in his mind were the rolls of blankets covering the dead, and the pools of dried blood on the floor of the house. How would he ever sleep again?

They waited. Then waited some more.

As the light rose in the east over the treetops, Chnals heard the creak of the old barn door. He jumped up. Papa stood in the doorway, his face ragged and shoulders bent. "Come, come, children. Come meet your new sister, little Anne. We will call her Anchen for now, because she is very young and small."

The sisters—except Helena, who still clutched little Maria—cheered and ran into the barn toward Mama. Chnals and Gerhard followed close behind them. The young woman who had helped Mama turned and beckoned them with her arm. She held the water bucket with something in it, but quickly whisked it away.

"Come, children," Mama called in a weak but happy voice. She sat on a pile of dirty blankets in the straw. Obviously the girls had not found clean blankets in the house. And then he saw her! A tiny baby wrapped in a shawl on his mother's lap. Suddenly a deep, warm, joyous sensation flooded his heart. Little Anchen. What a beautiful child. A miracle!

He ran outside to catch his breath. As he glanced toward the house, he saw the men, women, and children of their group standing in the side garden, hands folded and heads bowed. He walked toward them and stood beside a couple of the young men near the mounds of dirt.

One of the older men held a Bible and spoke."God bless these people. Please take them home to their eternal rest and peace, where there will be no more pain or grief."

Birth and death—joy and sorrow—the beginning and the end. All mixed together.

Chnals bowed his head and his eyes filled with tears

STORY 14
Arriving in Suworowka

ANNA

THE WIND RATTLED *the windows at the aunties' house. Dad's head snapped up. He rose from the table and shoved his plate of leftover* varenike *to the side. "It's getting dark. The radio says there's another storm coming. We need to go."*

"But how did you get to Suworowka? And how come the Mountain Tatars disappeared?" I asked, annoyed to have one more of Dad's stories chopped into fragments. I knew he was right to hurry, but I also knew he had a tendency not to complete his stories about Russia. He'd often leave them at the worst possible spots. Maybe he knew what he was doing. After all, my English teacher had taught the class to create tension at the end of each chapter of a book so as to excite our readers enough to turn the pages.

"I'll tell you when we get home."

I shrugged and shook my head as I pulled on my parka, wool hat, and gloves.

"I promise," Dad said, grabbing his jacket. He picked up my suitcase next to the door and headed out.

As we hurried toward our new shiny black Buick, the storm began to rage outside even harder, snow obscuring our vision. I pulled my blue parka tight around my body, swinging open the car door. The wind whipped at it, almost tearing it off.

"Hurry," Dad called to me as he started the car. Thank heaven, when he arrived at the aunties' farm, he had plugged it into an electrical outlet on the outside of the garage. It roared to life. In those days, block heaters could keep the engine warm enough to start even in fifty degrees below zero weather. Cars and trucks with electrical cords protruding from their grills were a common sight.

I pulled the car door shut behind me. Bending forward, I turned on the radio and sat back, my hands clasped tight. My whole body and even my teeth shivered. The announcer on the CBC station urged, "Stay home if you can! There's another storm coming in from North Dakota."

In my heart I knew I should have offered to stay at the aunties' for the weekend, but I really wanted—no, needed—to go home. At the age of fourteen and after two weeks in town, I missed my dog, Terry, and my parents intensely. Especially my mother. She had become my best friend after my sister moved to Winnipeg to go to nursing college.

As we drove, the storm seemed to ease and I let go of my seat. When we passed a giant million-dollar house near town, I saw my father shake his head.

"What's wrong, Dad?" I said.

He remained quiet for a while and I kept studying his face. At last he leaned back and shook his head again. "Anna," he said quietly. "That man makes a lot of money in his business selling cars and trucks. He should be giving half his money to the needy. Does he have any idea how blessed he is? Why does he need a big house like that? They say he and his wife have no children."

I finally understood where all those checks my dad wrote each month went. And why sometimes my best clothes, bought from the Hudson's Bay catalogue, disappeared to help young girls in our area.

And then suddenly a rare grin covered his face. "Of course, there are good things about money too! You asked me why the Mountain Tatars disappeared and left us alone. Thank goodness we were well off in Russia and we had rubles. Lots and lots of rubles. All the men in our group chipped in and gave the rubles to our guards from Kostek to bargain with the Tatars for our lives. According to your grandfather, the Tatars were very greedy young men. They took the money and let us go."

Abruptly the storm whipped up again. We were about halfway home and I clung to my seat, my jaw clenched, as the car lurched back and forth on the snow- and ice-covered gravel road. Silent, brow furrowed, Dad tightened his hands on the steering wheel. When we finally turned into our quarter-mile driveway, I let out a big breath. Thank heaven we were safe. Although my parents always carried big wool blankets, water, and food in the trunk of the car in winter, it was not uncommon to hear of people frozen to death while traveling during winter blizzards.

At home I dashed to my mother and hugged her tight. The familiar smell of fried potatoes and roasted rooster comforted me, and my whole body relaxed. I was home!

People say, "How did you know it was a roasted roaster, not a hen?"

I laugh. "You don't eat your hens! They lay eggs. And roosters? Well, they're bigger, they're delicious, and they are kind of useless, except for dinner . . . unless you like to see a tiny chicken in your eggs when you fry them.

After all the chores were done outside, my parents and I sat down at the table for homemade raspberry pie. When we finished, Dad turned to me, got up, and said, "I promised to finish my story, so let's go to the living room."

I glanced at Mom as she stood up and began to clear the table. She smiled and nodded. "Go," she said. I hurried after him and sat down next to Dad on our brown leather sofa as I so often had during my childhood.

CHNALS

Each day, a couple of the young men with flour sacks full of rubles and silver stood watch in the forest near the railroad, waiting for the *chug, chug* of the train. And each day Chnals and the others waited, ready to jump onto the train to Suworowka. They had run out of chickens to cook, and the milk cow had gone mostly dry. Even the flour that they found in the house was almost gone. The women had mixed it with water and made it into unleavened bread, as the Muslims had taught them.

Chnals could see the worry on his mother's face as she cradled little Anchen in her arms. Every couple of hours Anchen cried and Mama took her into one of the bedrooms. Then she'd close the door. And each time, Papa stood erect, hands grasped in the back, guarding the door.

The woman who had helped Mama give birth often went in with Mama or positioned herself next to Papa. "I'm so sorry," she whispered. "I wish I could help, but she has very little milk." Her face slumped and tears sprang into her eyes.

Each morning Papa and a couple of other men went out with their rifles to hunt, but with little success, except for a few birds and squirrels.

And then one day Wilhelm dashed into the yard, waving his arms and yelling, "Hurry! Come! We have a train. They're waiting for us."

Everyone grabbed their cloth bags and hurried down the quarter mile of forest trail to the train. The girls and Gerhard ran ahead, with Chnals in the rear. Papa scooped up little Anchen from Mama's arms, and Mama followed close behind.

At the train they climbed into one of the cattle cars and settled down in the straw, the women and children in the back, and the men near the door.

One of the men turned to the conductor and asked in Russian, "How far are we from Suworowka?"

His brow furrowed and he hesitated. Then he turned and slipped his arm around an elderly man as he helped him down onto the straw. At last he said, "Not far. Don't worry. We'll be there before evening. But you'll need to be quiet now. You never know who is listening."

Silence spread as the train lurched forward on the rails. Even Maria and little Anchen were quiet. He could hear Anchen slurp her thumb. Poor baby. She was hungry. But as soon as they arrived in Suworowka, they would have food. Lots and lots of food. He heard his stomach rumble and he tried to quiet it with his hand. However, it seemed to have a mind of its own.

After a while, Wilhelm and a couple of the older men sitting next to Papa and Chnals began to talk to each other in quiet voices. "I don't understand. Why do the Russians hate us so much that they want to kill us?" Wilhelm whispered. His voice sounded strained and sad.

Chnals leaned closer to the men so he could hear. He wanted to know the answer but he had never had the courage to ask the question. In a good German family, you just didn't ask about things like that!

"*Shh.* We can't talk now," one of the men whispered back as he glanced at Chnals.

Just then the conductor returned and Papa stopped him. "Can we talk to you?"

He hesitated. "I'm busy." But then he sat down next to the men, "Okay. For a minute." Papa leaned toward him, fidgeting with his hands. Chnals knew what that meant. Papa was about to ask the conductor something he wouldn't want anyone to hear. "Can you tell us if Suworowka is safe? Are the people okay there? We heard that many of the people from the Tereker Settlement have escaped to villages around Suworowka."

The conductor sighed, the furrows in his brow thickening. He tried to straighten his dirt-covered uniform and twisted his cap. At last he said, "I guess you need to know. You come at a bad time. Both the White and the Red Army are fighting here. The Red Army has come and is trying to take over the villages. They want to take over all of Russia. They're stealing everything and are killing all the men from the White Army. Suworoka is at the battlefront."

The men gasped. "Then we can't stop there!" Wilhelm exclaimed out loud. Several women on the other end of the car turned toward them.

Papa checked around, then shushed the men and leaned closer to the conductor. "We don't want to stop in Suworowka. Can't we just move on to Ukraine? We have family there. They'll take us in."

The conductor shook his head and looked in the direction of the women and children. "I'm sorry. The Red Army takes all the trains going north. The White Army can't protect you anymore. You will have to stay and wait."

Papa's face turned white and his jaw dropped. "But for how long?"

The conductor shrugged. "We don't know. Until someone wins. And right now it looks bad for the White Army."

Chnals hung his head as the truth filtered down into his chest and began to hurt. There would be no extra food. There would be no safety. They had been running, hiding, trying to escape, just to find themselves right back in the middle of the war.

The sun dipped down into the Caucasus Mountains to the west, just as the train slowed to a stop. The whistle blew loud and clear. Everybody hurried to pick up their bags and disembark. As they jumped down from the train, Chnals suddenly saw soldiers from the White Army rush toward them and grab the young men from the group. Wilhelm gasped and his face turned to stone. He struggled to free himself. But the soldiers hung onto him tight. He turned his face to his parents and yelled out in German. "Mama! Papa! *Auf wiedersehen. Bald!*" (Mother! Father! See you again. Soon!). His mother collapsed to the ground and began to wail. The other women gathered around her and bent down to comfort her.

In shock, Chnals stood still, jaw wide open, heart pounding, as he watched the soldiers seize all the men from their group, except the oldest ones. What was going on? Then they headed toward Papa and Chnals.

Two young soldiers grabbed Papa, but they ignored Chnals, who stood beside him. Papa struggled hard with his arms. "Stop! What are you doing?" he yelled in Russian.

One of the soldiers lifted his rifle to Papa's chest, and Papa stood still. The other soldier yanked at Papa's arm. "You are being conscripted into the White Army."

Papa looked into the man's eyes and shook his head, then pointed behind him. "Can't you see I have a wife and eight children, and the little one is only a few weeks old? I have to protect them and feed them. We are starving. Don't you understand?"

The soldier stared back at Papa, then slowly lowered his rifle. "We need more men. The Red Army is killing us all. We have no choice if we want this country to survive. That communist Lenin is taking over Russia. You are German and you have always supported the Czar. You have to serve."

Papa dipped his hand into a pants pocket and pulled out a roll of rubles.

"Here. Take this. I can't fight. I won't leave my family. But I'll do all I can to help you."

The young men stood in silence for a few seconds, looking at each other. Finally the older one nodded. "Okay. Give it to me." He held out his hand.

"No," Papa said. "On your honor, you promise me, I am free?"

The men looked at each other, nodded again, and the older placed his hand on his heart. The other soldier grabbed the roll of rubles and stuffed it into his pocket. Giant smiles crossed both of their faces. They bowed a little and took off running, chattering to each other.

Chnals watched the men retreat, then suddenly remembered Mama and the others. Were they okay? Quickly he turned around and saw Mama, face frozen in terror, staring at Papa. Her body shook so hard that little Anchen started to whimper. Gerhard and his sisters huddled together behind Mama.

Papa hurried toward them. "It's okay. It's okay. They'll leave us alone now."

"But where are we going to stay?" Mama whispered, her voice shaking as hard as her body.

Papa shrugged his shoulder. He hesitated, then said in a quiet voice, "We have to have faith. We have to be strong. God is in charge now." He turned around and strode to the entrance of the railway station.

We have to be strong! We have to be strong! How many times had Chnals heard those words before? He pulled back his shoulders, stood tall, and turned to help Mama.

And then he remembered. In just a few days, he would be thirteen years old. He was a man now.

They waited. Then waited some more. After about an hour, Papa hurried out of the train station, waving his arm at them. "Come, come," he called out.

Chnals turned to Mama, who nodded her head. He rushed out to meet Papa. An elderly man in a worn brown suit and big cap swung open the door, walked out, and stood behind Papa. He folded his hands and bowed his head just a little.

Papa smiled. "This is Mr. Peters. He and his family live here." The man reached out his hand and Chnals grasped it. "He's come to take us to the widow Derksen's farm in a village nearby. She has room for us."

Mr. Peters nodded and replied in German. "Yes, we have been at the train station every day, waiting for you all."

Waiting for them? Who was "we?" And how had they known that some of the settlers from the Tereker villages were coming? Chnals looked at Mr. Peters and Papa, wanting them to explain, but neither said a word.

Papa turned to Mr. Peters. "We hope to be on our way very soon. My parents live in Alexanderpol, Bakhmut, in Ukraine, We'll be safe there."

Mama walked to Papa's side and greeted the man, her voice breaking, "Thank you. Thank you so much. God bless you."

Papa reached for Anchen and looked deep into Mama's eyes. "God has answered our prayers."

Silent tears flooded Mama's cheeks as she handed Anchen to him.

STORY 15
The Widow Derksen's Farm

ANNA

SATURDAY MORNING I woke up and rushed to my bedroom window to check if the snow had stopped. Shoving away the pink cotton curtains, I groaned. *The snow swirled and spat at the window pane as though daring me to come near. Dark clouds whirled overhead. I could hear the wind whistle through the pine trees next to the barn that had now disappeared behind a white curtain. I took a deep breath and shook my head. I was only fourteen, but I knew better. I should not have insisted I come home for the weekend. There was no way I could get back to school on Monday without endangering my dad and me.*

But sometimes the days we fear most become treasured times. Because of the blizzard, besides feeding the animals and milking the cows, my parents and I spent most of the weekend huddled by the gas stove, drinking tea and trying to stay warm. Actually, the three days ahead became the weekend of many stories and many revelations.

I asked all the questions I had wondered about for years now. And best of all, Dad would swallow hard, look out the living room window into the storm, and nod. "Anna, it's a tough story. You know that. But you need to know our history so we never need to repeat it. You're in high school now. And a young woman."

I leaned back in my deeply overstuffed recliner and pulled at my blue jeans to help settle my legs under me. "Dad, I'm just curious. Do you know why the revolutionaries called themselves the Red Army? And the Czarists the White Army?"

Dad smiled and nodded. "Actually, the Red Army was named for the blood, shed by the working-class people against capitalism. And the name 'Whites' was used to describe those people loyal to the monarchy. That goes back to the French Revolution in 1789, when the monarchist forces took the white flag as their symbol."

"Did you ever find out why the people there in Suworowka knew you were coming?"

"Yes. Yes. Didn't I explain that?"

I shrugged. I certainly didn't recall.

"I heard Mr. Peters tell Papa before he dropped us at Mrs. Derksen's the day we arrived in Suworowka. Apparently, a lot of the villagers from the Tereker Settlement had already arrived there and had been sheltered by the people who lived near Suworowka. Some of our friends knew about us being thrown off the train. But they didn't know what had happened to us."

CHNALS

Slowly the horses clopped through a small village near Suworowka. Like the Tereker villages, houses next to barns lined up along a dirt street, with farm land stretching out behind each plot. Chnals gazed out over the dry prairie land, wishing, wishing, wishing, he were back home.

He jolted back to the present as Mr. Peters called out, "Whoa!" and eased his grip on the reins. The wagon slowed, then stopped at the front of a large, two-story house. On the front porch, an elderly woman wearing a black dress and a shawl covering her head, sat bent over in a rocking chair, her hands folded as though in prayer. She was obviously grieving.

Mr. Peters motioned toward the woman. "Mrs. Derksen," he said. "I'll go talk to her." He laid down the reins on the edge of the wagon and slowly rose from the wooden box he sat on.

Papa bent toward Mr. Peters. "Is she okay? What happened to Mr. Derksen?"

Mr. Peters swallowed hard and whispered, "Young men from the Red Army broke down the door and shot him in front of her. They stole everything they could. We're afraid she has lost her mind."

Chnals felt his throat tighten and anger flare through his body. Who were these Red Army soldiers anyway? He had read about Marx and communism in school, but this? What was wrong with these men? Were they all crazy?

Papa's face tightened into a glare and his jaw trembled, but he said nothing. Then he sighed and shook his head. "When did it happen?"

"A few days ago. Can you help her while you're here? She has no one. Her children live in Ukraine and the neighbors are struggling too,"

"Of course. Of course," Papa said. "The girls will cook and help her inside, and Chnals and I will take care of the animals."

Mama held little Anchen close and tightened the blanket around her. She glanced at Helena and Sara, and nodded.

"I'll go talk to her first. Then we'll get you settled. She has lots of room," Mr. Peters said as he climbed down over the front wheel.

Papa bent toward Mr. Peters and whispered, "We heard this area is now the *Rot/Weiss* (Red/White) front of the *Burgerkrieg* (civil war). Are they still fighting here?"

Mr. Peters shrugged and shook his head. "I don't think so. I think they've gone south."

Chnals took a deep breath and let go. They would be safe. His mind stretched into the future. He and Gerhard would have a room to themselves again. Maybe even a real bed. Like home. And soon they would be on their way to his grandparents in Ukraine. And he would finally meet his father's family and cousins. He could almost imagine them. And maybe, just maybe, his Oma and Opa Schmidt had survived and escaped to Ukraine as well!

An hour later, Chnals tiptoed down the stairs from his and Gerhard's new bedroom, and into the living room. Mama sat near Mrs. Derksen on the large blue sofa, holding her hand. He could hear Mama speak softly, but could catch only a few of the words. A stream of tears rolled down Mrs. Derksen's cheeks. He stood by the window and looked out, pretending not to listen. Then he heard Mama ask, "I just wondered. By any chance, did an older couple by the name of Schmidt come by here?"

Mrs. Derksen shook her head, "No, I don't think so. There've been many people from the Tereker Settlement come to the villages nearby, but no one by the name of Schmidt that I know of. Why?"

Mama's face drooped. "Oh, I just wondered. My parents."

Mrs. Derksen sat up and stroked Mama's arm. "I'm so sorry. Of course, I'm not sure. There were so many people . . . ." Her voice faded away.

Without a sound, Chnals snuck out of the front door and stepped onto the wooden porch. He looked around and took a deep breath, filling his thirsty lungs with the clean country air. Flat land, covered in winter wheat stretched, it seemed, for miles behind him.

Suddenly he heard Papa's voice yell, "Chnals! Chnals! Come help. Quick!"

He gasped and yanked his head toward the voice. Papa stood by the giant barn door near the rear of the house, frantically waving his arm at Chnals. Oh, no! What now? Then Papa turned and ran back into the barn.

Chnals dashed after him. A few pigs wandered about outside, but as he entered the barn, his nostrils stung with the stench of dead flesh, old urine, and poop. Papa shoved a large bucket with water into his hands. And then he saw it. Empty troughs. No water. No food. Several dead chickens, strewn about the front end of the barn, lay rotting on the dirt floor. Others still sat on their straw nests, heads hanging low. At the other end of the barn he heard a loud moan, and he saw a cow stumble to her feet. A few others lay gasping on the floor. One horse. That was it. Obviously the rest of the animals had been stolen by the Red Army.

Chnals rushed about filling the troughs with water, but the chickens didn't move. He stared at them, then turned to Papa who had come up behind him. "Papa. Why aren't they coming to drink?"

"Here, Chnals. Grab a hen and do what I do." Without explaining, Papa snatched one chicken off her nest and dipped her beak into the trough of water. The hen gulped at the water and tried to flutter away, but collapsed into Papa's arms. He placed her gently back onto her nest.

After the chickens were watered, Papa grabbed the pail. "Come, come." He hurried to the horse, now lying panting on the straw. Slowly Papa filled his hand with water and placed it close to the horse's mouth. A thirsty gray tongue swished out and gulped down the water. Then, groaning, he laid his head back on the straw.

Chnals nodded. He knew what to do. He filled his two hands with water from the pail and trembling, he dropped down beside one of the cows. The cow's abdomen heaved as it lifted its head and turned toward him, looking into his eyes. Quickly she licked the water from his hands and checked for more.

"Should I give her more?" he called to Papa, who now knelt next to one of the other cows.

"Not too much," Papa called back. "Just a little to start with, so they don't get sick."

When they finished, they placed a pail filled with water outside, for the pigs, and hurried into the house. His stomach growled as the welcome odor of warm bread met him at the door. They had eaten nothing since leaving Suworowka. He ran to the kitchen only to see his brother and sisters sitting on benches around a large wooden table, chattering and eating sliced 'black-bread' with onions.

He stood back and watched, but said nothing. What happened to that amazing dinner of chicken and mashed potatoes he'd imagined when they first arrived? Oh, well . . . . Finally

Chnals swung his legs over the bench next to him. He grabbed a piece of warm bread with fried onions and gulped it down. He smacked his lips. Delicious! Of course, anything would taste good if you felt as if you were starving.

After dinner, Papa tapped Chnals on the shoulder. "We need to get enough food for the animals for tomorrow."

Lantern in hand, Papa steered Chnals to the barn again and hunted for a set of shears and a scythe. When they finally found them stuck under straw and barrels, they cut some of the long grass and winter wheat in the back yard, well into darkness. The moon stared back at him again, but Chnals smiled as he stacked the grass by the side of the barn. He was safe. No moon would ever scare him again!

That night, for the first time in months, Chnals crawled into a real bed with real linens. Still in his dirty pants and long-sleeved shirt, he fell sound asleep.

STORY 16
The Red Army Soldiers

ANNA

IT WAS SUNDAY *morning and the storm still raged on. There would be no relief at least for another day. The announcer on the CBC station warned people not to go outside unless it was an emergency. Several people had already been reported missing on the road. I just hoped the people had enough gas and blankets and water to keep them alive. At least I was at home, safe for now.*

I slept late that morning, and Mom knocked lightly on my bedroom door. She peeked into the bedroom. "Are you awake? It's almost time for lunch!"

I bolted upright in bed and checked my watch, "Oh, my gosh, Mom! Why did you let me sleep so long? What about the chickens?" I could hear her laugh and she closed the door. Quickly I jumped out of bed and dressed in my jeans and my long-sleeved purple shirt. Next I yanked on my brown leather boots, now lined up by the door. I brushed my short dark curls and staggered to the bathroom. After washing my face, I pulled on my parka and ran out the door into the storm to feed the chickens.

My mother called after me, "Anna, no. It's okay. I fed the chickens. Come in and eat lunch with us. I've got your favorite. Chicken salad sandwiches and pickled watermelon."

Yum. I felt my stomach rumble.

We couldn't go to church, so my dad read his favorite passage in the Bible to us: Psalm 121. It was the same passage that their minister had read to the villagers on the Sunday the settlers had arrived in Kasi Jurt, the Muslim village nearest them. And after they had watched all their homes go up in smoke.

His voice broke as he read, "I will lift up mine eyes unto the hills from whence cometh my help. My help cometh from the Lord who made heaven and earth."

I shook my head. How could my dad still have such deep faith in God after all they had been through? And then I remembered what he and Grandpa so often said."Yes, we went through the very depth of pain and grief. But God always led us to such kind people who helped us everywhere we went. How can we forget? Even now we thank God every day."

Dad put down the well worn Bible on the table and, without me asking, he continued telling the stories of Russia during the revolution.

CHNALS

Chnals sat on the windowsill of his second-story bedroom window, staring into the darkness. How long had it been since they had come to live with Frau Derksen? Two weeks? Three weeks? Maybe more. He had lost track of time.

Each day the family waited for news that the Red Army had

left the area and they could finally board the train to Ukraine. But each day, no news. Just work on the fields. Feed and water the animals. Collect the eggs. Milk the cows.

Once in a while, the neighbors brought a roast chicken for their dinner, and they added potatoes from the now wilting garden. The rest of the time, Mama and the girls made cottage cheese, *varenike*, bread, fried onions, and scrambled eggs.

With Mama's constant companionship, Mrs. Derksen now smiled every once in a while, especially as she rocked baby Anchen in her arms, or danced around with Maria. He had even heard her laugh last night. What a miracle!

Often Mama and Mrs. Derksen grabbed a couple of metal bowls and together walked into the back yard to pick *loditz*, a common edible weed in the area. Then they cooked it with potatoes, carrots, and parsley to make it into soup. Chnals's stomach growled. He could feel the pounds drain from his body, and he knew Mama worried about feeding little Anchen. She was only a month old. But Mama never complained about anything. That was just who Mama was.

During the evenings, Mama and Mrs. Derksen and the girls sewed and embroidered pillow cases and dresses. The oldest girls took turns reading stories to the group and bouncing and rocking Anchen and Maria to sleep.

He glanced down at his dirty shirt that he had worn to bed. It had come as a big surprise to the entire family that the villages here had no artesian wells like they had in the Tereker Settlement. Only rain water that ran off the roof into a cistern, during a storm. And there had been very little rain the last winter—no clean water left for baths or to wash their dishes or clothes. Most of the time Mama and his sisters used the water two or three times, and then he and Papa gave it to the pigs.

He sighed. Maybe this morning they would finally leave.

At last he pulled shut the flour-sack curtain and snuck back to bed next to Gerhard. He covered himself with the handmade knitted blanket, so much like the one Oma had made for him. It had disappeared somewhere on the train when they had been forced to run into the forest to evade the army. Suddenly his throat tightened, and the image of his grandparents flashed in his mind. Oma. Opa. He cringed and his heart ached. Where were they now? Were they still alive?

"Stop thinking," he muttered to himself. If only he could shut off the memories and sleep. But nightmares of angry men and monsters hacking them all into tiny pieces haunted him night after night.

Chnals woke with a start. The sound of horses' hooves and voices of men echoed through his second-story bedroom window.

Gerhard sat straight up in bed next to him and gasped. "Chnals. What's going on? Are they coming for us?"

Still dressed in his wrinkled shirt, gray from washing with dirty water, Chnals rushed to the window. In the drab, half-breaking dawn, he saw several horses gallop onto the yard, dust flying behind them. Men jumped off their saddles, rifles in hand. Forgetting about Gerhard, Chnals ran out of the room to warn Papa. He heard Gerhard's stocking feet thump behind him.

In a gruff voice Papa called up from the bottom of the stairs. "It's nothing. Go back to sleep, boys. It's just the neighbors." Then he strode toward the front door.

Chnals turned and saw Gerhard hanging onto the rail. "It's nothing," Chnals echoed his father with a faint smile, pretending all was well, for Gerhard's sake. Yes, once again he had to be strong. How many times had that phrase popped up into his mind? It had an automatic ring to it by now. Quickly, he led his brother to their room. Gerhard jumped into bed, covered himself from head to toe with his own little blanket, and fell asleep.

Chnals trembled as he leaned back onto his feather mattress. Something had gone wrong again. He could feel the danger deep in his gut, and his heart sank. Although he closed his eyes, his mind kept racing and his body remained on alert.

'It's nothing!' Where had he heard those words before? Yes. At home, from his father. That night before the Tatars had attacked. He had thought, had hoped, had prayed they were safe here in Suworowka, But now?

About an hour later, still on alert, Chnals heard the hooves of the horses clop away. And soon after, Papa stole into the bedroom and beckoned to him. "We need to talk," Papa whispered, and then hurried out of the room. Chnals flung his blanket to the side of the bed. Pulling on his black wool pants and leather boots, he rushed down the stairs behind Papa, out toward the barn.

The once dark sky, now flooded by sunlight, began to glow in the east, lighting up the miles of green grass and winter wheat. But all he saw was danger.

As they entered the barn, Papa pointed to the two barrels next to the chicken nests. They sat down and Papa looked down toward the straw. His hands shook. Finally he said in an urgent but quiet voice, "Chnals, you are thirteen now. You need to know what is going on. Lenin, the head of the new government has opened all the prisons in the country, and many of the prisoners have joined the Red Communist Army. They are looting and stealing everything. They will be here any day." He hesitated and cleared his throat. "They want our women."

Chnals stared into his father's eyes. "Will we fight?"

Papa shook his head. "If we fight, we'll all die. The neighbors have decided we must work together and help each other as much as we can. We'll all try to protect the women and children." He paused. "Chnals . . . you know, if anything happens to me . . . " His words faded into the distance and he swallowed several times.

Chnals bent his head and nodded. Yes, he knew what Papa meant.

Papa turned and stroked the red feathers of the hen lying in the straw next to him. Then he straightened and rose. "Come. It's time. We must have faith."

Chnals's throat tightened and his legs trembled. Faith? How could you have faith after all that had happened? God had deserted them. Why was this happening?

At last he got up and followed Papa. He took a deep breath. Suddenly the foul odor of dung swept into his lungs and he doubled over, struggling not to throw up.

"Get out of the way!" one of the Red soldiers screamed as he swung his arm out at Chnals and punched him in the chest. Chnals stumbled to the kitchen floor. "Get out of here and don't come back!" The soldier kicked him in the ribs with his black leather boot.

Several soldiers in Red Army uniforms leaned back from the large kitchen table and cheered. Helena and Sara stared at the man, then ran toward Chnals. The man slapped the girls across their faces, picked up Chnals as though he was merely a small feather pillow, and threw him out of the back door. "Go feed our horses. Now!" he yelled and slammed the door.

Papa rushed out of the evening shadows next to the barn. "Chnals, Chnals are you all right?" He clenched his fists and his eyes flared with anger.

Quickly Chnals straightened and stood up tall. "I'm okay. He didn't hurt me." The last thing he needed now was for Papa to attack the soldiers. They would kill the whole family.

Papa stepped back and took several deep breaths. He held onto the beam by the side of the porch, but didn't move. A deep scowl lingered on his face. At last he said, "Are the others okay? Where is Mama?"

Chnals turned to evade Papa's eyes. He had better be careful what he said. He calmed his voice. "Yes. Helena and Sara are cooking roast pork for the men's dinner. And Mama and the others are hiding in the attic, as usual."

Papa stared into the darkening distance. "The men don't want us around. You know that."

Chnals nodded.

"They just want the young women to take care of them." Papa began to pace back and forth.

Through the kitchen window Chnals saw the kerosene lamp flame up and he caught a glimpse of the terrified look on Helena's face. He hung his head and his voice trembled. "Papa, I'm sorry. I know it's my duty, but I don't know what to do to keep the girls and Mama safe. There are too many soldiers. Too many rifles." He swallowed hard. "I tried." Tears flooded his eyes. Some nights he heard Helena and Mama scream into the silence, but no one spoke about it the next day. And he dared not ask. But he knew. The guilt weighed like a large rock on his chest.

Papa suddenly stopped and turned to him. "No. No. You did nothing wrong. We can't do anything if we all want to live. God will take care of us. You'll see."

Chnals closed his eyes and sighed. He tried to believe, but

he wasn't nearly as convinced as Papa. Where was God when they needed Him?

Just then he heard a laugh. Two soldiers burst through the barn door, one holding a flopping hen by the feet. No head. Blood dripped from the neck. Though the soldiers had only been there a month, they had already killed a couple of the pigs, a calf, and several of the hens. The family occasionally got the leftovers, but soon there would be no more eggs or milk.

He caught a glimpse of the red star on one of the soldier's hats as the men strode past them. He would never forget that red star. One of the soldiers shoved open the back door, and hurried inside, blood dripping onto the kitchen floor. He thrust the hen into Helena's hand.

"Come," Papa said. "It's time." Head bent, Papa led the way to the barn. "It's time to feed the animals and milk the cows."

Chnals picked up a pail half full of dirty water. With the soldiers and their horses using most of the water, it would not be long before it was gone. And then what?

Chnals leaned back on the large metal shovel and took a deep breath of sunshine. He needed to stop for a minute and rest after spending the last couple of hours digging weeds out of the cabbage and onion patch.

Another month had passed. It was now June and a new crop of vegetables had grown to almost full height. He shook his head and frowned. Still no change. Every evening at dusk, several soldiers, dressed in their filthy gray uniforms, galloped onto the yard and demanded dinner. At night they slept in the barn on the straw. By now the soldiers had stolen all their valuables except what Mama and Papa kept on their bodies. The rats and lice had invaded not only the barn, but also the house. Each morning, after the soldiers rode off to battle, Papa and Chnals grabbed up the straw and burned it in the kitchen stove, not only to heat the house and cook the food, but also to rid the place of lice and disease. Thank heaven it had finally rained, but there was still no water for baths or to wash their clothes.

Without thinking, Chnals swept his hand over his short, stubbled hair. Only a few days ago Mama had grabbed a pair of sharp scissors from Mrs. Gertsen's sewing kit sitting on the old treadle sewing machine in Mama and Papa's bedroom, and snipped off all the kids' hair, close to their scalps. His sisters screamed and cried as their long hair, filled with lice, tumbled to the floor. Then Mrs. Derksen cut Mama's hair and Mama cut hers. Chnals had noticed that all the girls and the women looked down each time they passed a mirror. When they did look up, their faces wrinkled as though in shame. He understood. He had never seen Mama or Helena with short hair, never mind cut to the scalp. He could barely look at the girls without avoiding their eyes.

A twig snapped behind him and he jerked to alert. *What was that?* Maybe just one of the wild pigs that roamed about at night. But without thinking, he clenched his fists, raised them and wheeled around. A small shadow ran toward him through the newly leafed-out aspen trees and wildflowers near the barn. Was it a soldier? Then a blond-haired boy about six, dressed in dark shirt and pants, burst through the trees and long grass. Chnals sighed with relief. It was only one of the neighborhood boys. The boy gasped and slumped to the dirt path near the barn.

Chnals rushed toward him "Otto! What's wrong?"

Panting, Otto raised his head and stared into his eyes. "Mama. She's burning up! We need help!"

Quickly Chnals picked Otto up by the arms. He carried the sobbing boy to the porch and dumped him onto one of the steps. "You sit here. I'll get Papa right now." He dashed into the house and called out in a panicked voice, "Papa! Papa!"

Moments later both Papa and Mama came running out of the kitchen. "What's wrong?" Mama called.

"It's Otto. His mother is very ill with a fever."

Mama and Papa looked at each other, mouths open, for a moment. Then Mama nodded and Papa took off running toward the road.

He would need some help to lift Mrs. Hiebert. "I'll go help him," Chnals called out to Mama as he ran for the steps.

"No, no." Mama called back in a commanding voice. "You stay here with Otto."

Chnals stopped and took a deep breath. Now what was wrong? Papa used that voice, but Mama never did.

Otto, his face covered with his hands, rocked back and forth as he sat on the wooden porch steps. Chnals knelt down next to him and placed his hand gently on his back. Poor kid. How could he help him? Then he remembered the large ball he and Gerhard had found in the attic and had left by the side of the house. At last he said, "Hey Otto. You like to play ball?"

Otto's face lit up and he smiled.

Chnals jumped up and ran to get the ball. He kicked it on the grass toward the porch. "Come on!" he shouted. "The barn door is the goal."

Otto dashed toward the ball and sent it flying with his foot. Chnals pretended to tussle with Otto for the ball, but Otto shoved him away and kicked it toward the barn. "I won. I won," he shouted as he raised his arms to the sunny blue sky.

Chnals clapped his hands. "Good job," he called out and ran to fetch the ball for another round. For the first time in months, he felt as though he were back at his village on the Terek, laughing and playing with his friends.

Minutes later Mama came out with what looked like a large dish filled with cookies. She handed one to Otto and then one to Chnals. Piroshky! Apple slices rolled up in dough and baked. His favorite dessert. Still warm. Probably Mama had baked them for the soldiers, but she had made enough for all of them. The rest of the children followed Mama and lined up on the porch.

Maria, now three, jumped with glee. "Persky! Persky" she shouted in her child voice.

About two hours later, Chnals, picking tomatoes in the garden next to the house, heard a horse gallop onto the driveway. Papa jumped down from the homemade saddle of burlap and rope. Slowly he headed toward Chnals, his face sullen. Chnals grabbed his bowl full of tomatoes and peas and strode toward Papa.

The door slammed and Mama ran out of the house. "Is she okay?" she called out.

Papa hurried toward her, then stopped. He bit his lip. "Where is Otto?"

"Inside. The kids are playing hide-and-seek with him. They're having fun!"

Finally Papa shook his head. "She's dead."

Mama gasped and her face turned white. "What happened?"

"Typhus. The whole family is sick, except Otto and one of his sisters. Otto's father's gone. He's fighting in the White Army, and no one knows where he is."

Chnals wanted to scream. He knew about typhus. People in the Tereker villages had struggled with typhus during a flood when he was little, and before the settlers had dug the canals.

Mama collapsed into the rocker on the porch. "How come? Did the army bring it?"

Papa nodded. "The lice." He turned toward Mama. "I talked

to several of the neighbors. We'll meet this afternoon before the soldiers come back. Lots of people in the village are getting ill. We need to work out a way to make sure everyone is taken care of."

Mama swallowed hard and stood up. "I'll help. And I know Mrs. Gertsen will too."

Papa's body jerked to alert. "No. You can't! You'll get sick. What about Maria and the baby?"

Mama touched him gently on the arm. "Helena is sixteen now and she can take care of the others." Then she stood up tall. "I have to go. We'll take Otto and his sister into our place for now."

Each day Chnals or Papa took the one horse remaining in the barn after the army left in the early morning, and hitched it to the small black buggy near the house. Both Mama and Mrs. Gertsen climbed inside and rode to the local school. Many of the sick were housed on the floors, huddling on thick woolen blankets. And each day Helena and Sara took care of the younger sisters and Gerhard, as well as Otto and his sister, while Papa and Chnals worked with the other men in the village, cutting and threshing winter wheat. Then in the morning and evening the men gathered to take care of all the animals in the village.

And each day the family stood with heads bowed as several wagons rumbled by the front of the Gertsen farm, carrying bodies to be buried at the gravesite near the church down the road.

Many soldiers fell ill as well, and demanded the villagers take care of them. Chnals and Papa served the sick soldiers their dinner in the barn and took care of their horses. Often Chnals heard them laugh and brag about the wins on the battlefield, even as their friends died next to them. *What was wrong with these men? Did they have no heart?*

But in the evening, when the soldiers returned, they buried their dead in the back fields and marked their graves with large wooden stick crosses.

Often in the early morning after the soldiers had left for the day, Chnals found his parents and Mrs. Gertsen in the living room, praying and reading the Martin Luther Bible. The children gathered around them in silence and listened.

And then Mama got typhus. And the world stood still. Would she live? What would the family do without her? Could the girls function on their own? Only Papa was allowed into her room to serve her and bathe her with the cold, wet towels Helena prepared. Chnals could see the worry lines deepen in his father's face.

Sometimes he heard his sisters argue as they weeded the garden and prepared the meals for the soldiers and the family. He would hold his breath as Papa watched at the door. But eventually the girls would burst into laughter. And Chnals let go. They were growing up too.

When Mama's fever finally broke and she was able to eat, Sara and Justina rushed about to cook some borscht and butter a giant piece of fresh bread, just like Mama loved it. Helena strode into the kitchen and shooed the girls away."No, no. Let me. Not so much."

"But she's hungry!" Justina scolded.

"I said NO!' Helena demanded. "People die if they eat too much while they're getting well." She scooped out a little soup in a bowl and cut the bread in half. "There. That's enough. Justina, you take it to her."

Each day Chnals watched to make sure Mama improved. And then one day a weary-looking, sallow, and much thinner Mama appeared at the door to the bedroom and smiled.

Late one afternoon in September, a Red Army soldier on horseback raced to the barn, jumped off his horse, and ran inside. Moments later Chnals and Papa, standing on the porch, heard a cheer so loud they would never forget. Still yelling, arms raised, all the soldiers, including the ones who were still ill, rushed outside, mounted their horses, and dashed away. Without saying a word, Papa ran to the barn. Chnals hurried after Papa, but before he could enter, the door opened and Papa, on horseback, galloped off after the soldiers. Chnals stared after him. What had happened?

About two hours later Papa returned and strode into the kitchen. He looked at Mama. "Are Maria and little Anchen asleep?" Mama nodded as though she knew what was about to happen. He nodded back "Come, let's all go and sit in the living room. There is news."

Mama glanced at Mrs. Derksen and they both gathered the children into the living room. Chnals followed the others and sat down cross-legged next to the sofa near Mama.

Papa paced back and forth and then stood up in front of the darkening living room window. He folded his hands behind him and with a steady voice said, "The Red Army has won and the front is moving south. The White Army has been defeated."

Mrs. Derksen covered her face with her hands and began to sob. "No, no! That can't be true. God would not let that happen! They killed my husband and so many people. What will happen to us now? Will they take away all our land and steal all our animals like they said?"

Mama hurried to place her arm around Mrs. Derksen. She was right. It wasn't fair.

Everyone stood in silence for a while. At last Mrs. Derksen whispered to Papa, "Do you think the Red Army has taken over

Ukraine? We haven't had any news from our families for a long time. Are my children all dead too?" She began to sob again.

"No, no," Papa said, though his voice did not sound convincing. "Everything will be fine. The Red Army is no longer using the trains. I talked to one of the conductors. He said we can leave for Ukraine now."

"Really?" Gerhard stood up, deep relief written on his young face.

"Yes. Really." Papa said smiling.

The girls rose as one and clapped, cheered, and danced around the room. They chattered as though nothing could ever go wrong again, making plans of a wonderful future. Soon they would all be in Ukraine at Grandma and Grandpa Unger's house. They would go back to school and play tag and hide-and-seek. And have fun with the cousins whom they had never met. Most of all, they would all be safe again.

Chnals bent his head and closed his eyes. If only. But he doubted. Safe? Not likely. Was Mrs. Derksen right? Had the Red Army taken over Ukraine too? Had the communists stolen all the land from the Germans as they had promised the peasants? They had heard no news from their families for several months. He wondered—was he becoming wiser with age, or just more cynical? He had learned in these last eight months that he could never count on the future. Nothing seemed to be in his control anymore.

STORY 17

Preparing to Leave

ANNA

THE STORM HAD *finally stopped during the night. Just before lunch on Monday, I pulled on my snow pants, my blue parka, wool hat, and high-topped boots, and cautiously ventured out onto the three-foot-high drifts near the house, now hard as ice. The sun shone on the sparkling snow and the air smelled fresh, crisp, and clean. I took a deep breath and gulped as I felt my lungs turn into ice cubes. Quickly I checked the temperature gauge just outside the porch. Thirty-five degrees below zero! Ouch. I ran inside and wound a heavy wool scarf around my neck and face.*

Then I grabbed a large bucket full of milled grain from the nearby barn and hurried to feed the chickens. As always, the hens greeted me, squawking and clucking, as I slammed the door behind me and poured the grain into their bins. Fortunately Dad had turned on the electric heating lamps and the barn felt nice and warm. I gathered the eggs from the nests and placed them into the now empty bucket. Then I sat down on one of the perches and watched the hens scurry about and gobble down their food, while I contemplated my now "sorry" life.

I had already missed a day of school and I wasn't at all sure I would be back on Tuesday. It was a good thing Mom had called the school secretary and the people I lived with to explain, so there should be no problem when I returned. But I could only imagine how overwhelmed I'd be all week, trying to catch up. I loved reading, algebra and geometry. But world history? No! And each week our history teacher assigned long essays to be completed by the next Monday.

Just then I heard the tractor chug and brum outside, and I jumped to my feet. I knew Dad and two of our neighbors had been out most of the morning, plowing the two feet of hard drifts on the mile of dirt road leading to the gravel county highway. Had they finished? Had they succeeded in clearing the snow enough to drive on with the cars? I missed my friends. Excited, I imagined myself tomorrow, early morning, hurrying into the car with my suitcase packed with clean clothes. And a big cardboard box full of goodies Mom always filled for me to snack on during the next two weeks.

That evening, as we had all weekend, we gathered in the living room after supper to listen to the news, drink tea, and talk. I was eager to hear Dad tell the story of their arrival in Ukraine as he had promised last night. But most of all I wanted to know if Oma and Opa Schmidt from Village #9 had survived. How should I ask so as not to cause Dad more pain?

I hesitated for a long time, playing different scenarios in my mind. At last I blurted out the question. "You know, Dad," I said. "You've never told me about your grandparents Schmidt from the Tereker Settlement. Did they escape that day your homes were burned in 1918? Did you ever see them again? I've never met them."

Dad frowned and leaned forward in his blue upholstered chair near the fireplace. He placed his hands closer to the fire and rubbed them together. Instead of answering my question he launched into the story about their final escape to Ukraine in a matter-of-fact way.

CHNALS

The day after the soldiers left and the people felt sure the Red Army would not return, all the men from the Tereker villages who had escaped to the Suworowka area, met at one of the schools. When Papa returned, he and Mama hurried into the garden, now green with cabbage, onions, peas, and cucumbers. Chnals checked the window and saw Mama smile and nod her head. He sighed with relief. Everything would be okay.

Minutes later, Mama and Papa walked into the house and gathered the family, except little Anchen, Maria, and Otto and his sister, into the living room again. Mrs. Derksen stood by the door, rocking Anchen, now almost five months old, in her arms.

Papa sat down in the old oak rocker near the window and rocked the chair back and forth. Bright sunlight beamed through the single glass pane. He smiled, glanced at the window, and moved the chair away, closer to Mama. At last he said, "Children. Our plans are simple. We're going to help the people here finish up with their crops, and then we're on our way to Ukraine to Grandma and Grandpa Unger's house."

Sara rose to her feet with a stunned look on her face. "But how about Otto and his sister? Everyone in their family is dead! We can't leave them behind. They have no one."

Mama gently tapped Sara on her back and said in a soft voice. "It's okay. Don't worry. It's all taken care of. The children who have no one here are coming with all of us on the train to Ukraine. They are part of our families now."

Chnals heard what sounded like a stifled sob and turned toward the living room door. Mrs. Derksen, head bent, rushed out of the room in her long dark dress and disappeared, with Anchen still in her arms.

Mama bent over as though in pain, and covered her face. Quickly she rose and ran after Mrs. Derksen, calling, "Wait! Wait! Elanna! We need to talk. You can come with us! Your children and grandchildren all live in Ukraine."

Chnals felt a deep ache in his chest. Of course. A sudden memory of when they first arrived flashed into his mind. Mrs. Derksen, crumpled over in her rocker on the porch. Her husband had been killed by the Red Army soldiers, and now Mama, her best friend, and little Anchen, her purpose for living, would soon be gone. How could she handle life on her own? Yes. Why couldn't she come with them to Ukraine where her children lived? But his answer never came in words.

Each day Chnals and Papa with the men and teenage boys from the Tereker Settlement gathered to help the men from the villages around Suworowka thresh the wheat, then bind the straw, and plow the fields. Tomorrow they would sow the winter wheat for the next crop. And then it would be time to leave.

Chnals, exhausted, slumped down onto the pile of straw he pitched into the wagons as they rumbled by. He stared into the distance longing to see Mount Elbrus. Soon they would be gone and then, would he ever see his mountain again? His security, his home? According to Papa, Ukraine stretched almost a thousand *werst* north. Would he ever come back here?

He heard a horse's hooves gallop toward him and stop. Jumping to his feet, he whirled around. It was only Papa. Slowly he took a deep breath and relaxed.

"Come Chnals. Hurry," Papa called out to him. "Come with me and let's join all the other men. We have to make plans. It's time to leave."

Chnals shook his head in surprise as though trying to wake from a dream. Was Papa actually including him? He ran toward his father who pulled him up on his horse. "Where are we going?" he asked.

"To the school. All the men from the Tereker Settlement who will be leaving with us to Ukraine are meeting at the school in just a few minutes." They galloped away across the plowed fields and toward the dirt and clay road nearby.

When they finally arrived at the school, Papa and Chnals jumped down. Papa tied the horse to a post. Chnals waited. As he turned around, Papa grasped Chnals by his shoulder and looked squarely into his eyes. "Listen. Listen to everything the men say. You are a man now, and you need to know what is going on. Just in case."

Chnals felt a blush cover his cheeks and his heart pound. A man? Was he ready?

Quickly Papa headed toward the door of the old wooden school. Outside, about twenty or thirty men stood in a group, all dressed in dirty torn shirts and pants. As usual the young men gathered on one side of the circle, and the older men gathered on the other side. Quietly Chnals snuck in behind the other young men. No one seemed to notice him.

After a couple of minutes, Mr. Tabert, the miller, from the Tereker villages, unlocked the door to the school and shoved it open. He beckoned to the men with his arm. "Come now. We need to hurry."

The men followed him and slipped into the chairs next to the homemade desks. Chnals sat down and started to fiddle around with the small ink bottle on his desk. Suddenly his mind flashed back to his last day at school. He felt his heart thump hard as he returned to the terror that had wracked his body when the teacher confirmed that a thousand man army was dashing down the Caucasus Mountains to rob and kill them. He closed his eyes and took a deep slow breath as Mama had taught him. The fear flowed into nothingness as he breathed out. Count your blessings. It was truly a miracle that his entire family was still alive.

"There's a train coming through from Chassow Jurt to Ukraine the day after tomorrow. It is believed there will be room for all of us," Mr. Tabert said. The group cheered and clapped. "We all know that the Red Army has stolen most of our valuables so it won't take long to pack. We have told the women, and they are already busy gathering food and baking bread. And we will take bottles of water. The trip should take only a couple of days. Are there any questions?"

One of the middle-aged men from Village #6 stepped forward. "How much will it cost for my family? There are five of us. The soldiers stole all of our rubles, my wife's jewelry, and everything else we brought." A murmur ran through the group. Several men nodded.

"We'll help each other as we always have, right?" Mr. Tabert said in a commanding voice. Several older men nodded.

Chnals glanced at Papa who gritted his teeth and stared out into nowhere, as though he hadn't heard the question. When they first arrived, he had seen Mama and Mrs. Gertsen sew several small bags made of one of Mrs. Gertsen's old skirts, fill them with jewelry and rubles, and tie them around their bellies. Then when the Red Army moved into the farm, they tucked the bags under their clothes. They wore them continuously, night and day. In all those months he had never seen his parents and Mrs Gertsen remove the bags from their bodies. He had wondered why, but now it all made sense.

"We'll take care of it," Mr. Tabert continued. "Our friends here in Suworowka have promised to help us. If there is anyone who doesn't have enough rubles left to get on board, please come to me. Are there any other questions?"

One of the younger husky men with tousled blond hair Chnals had never met strode to the front of the group and said in a worried voice, "My wife and I have three little children. What's going to happen to us when we get to Ukraine? We have no close family there. A man in the village we are staying at said Lenin and the Red Army are taking over Ukraine as well as the rest of Russia."

Several men gasped and the noise in the room turned into an uncontrolled buzz.

Mr. Toews, the minister, who sat at the back of the school, rose slowly from his desk and headed to the front, next to the man. He hesitated, then said, "Men. It's time to talk about something most of us have not wanted to talk about. But it's time. The new government."

The older men looked sullen, nodded, and murmured to each other.

Mr. Toews straightened, stepped forward, and continued. "There has been talk of communism for a long time, but we haven't paid much attention to it. We thought they could never get rid of Czar Nicholas. Not with the White Army protecting him. But now Lenin's men have killed him. And Lenin and the Red Army are taking over everything. We don't know if we have any freedom's left, or what they will do with us."

Mr. Taber stood up again. "Mr. Toews is right. Most of us should have read about Marx and his ideas but we didn't think we would ever need to know. How many of you understand what communism is all about?"

Chnals and some of the younger men raised their hands.

"Chnals, you are still in school. Did you study about Marx?" Mr. Toews, the minister said, stretching his rough and weathered hand toward him.

Chnals nodded.

"Can you tell us what you learned?"

Chnals gulped and tried to fade into the desk, just as he had when the teacher called on him at school. Why had he raised his hand? Be strong. Be strong, he kept muttering inside his mind. You are a man now.

Papa looked at him, smiled, and nodded.

Chnals straightened and pretended he was a man. He strode up to the front next to the minister. "Yes, we studied a little bit about Marx and communism in history class. He was just some German philosopher with strange ideas about everybody being equal and the state owning everything. And we learned Lenin liked his ideas."

The minister placed his hand on Chnals's arm and said. "Thank you Chnals." He turned and addressed the group. "We know it's been a year now since Lenin took over Russia. He got Russia out of World War I. But then, like we have seen here, the Red Army is winning everything."

He folded his hands and looked down for a moment. Then he addressed the men again. "Did anyone else read about Marx and Lenin?" Some shook their heads. A few nodded. "Can any of you younger ones tell us exactly what Marx believed?"

A young man about twenty, with longish, slicked back hair got up and marched to the front next to the minister, his dirty pants nearly sliding off his now skinny frame. "Marx thought that the government should make sure there would be no social classes.

No rich people or poor people. The land and everything would belong to the state and the public. And the government would pay and treat everyone the same. That way all the people would have the same opportunities. No one would be poor or hungry."

A middle-aged man with curly brown hair, wet from sweat, got up. "Isn't that what Jesus wanted when he said to leave our homes and go help the poor and sick? Didn't he say *all* people are children of God? It's wrong for a few to own everything while others starve and have no homes."

Several of the young men glowered at him. One of them stomped his feet, and shouted, "In plain words what you are saying is that they will take away all our land, our homes, our animals and everything we have like they did at the Tereker Settlement. And let all the German people starve! Just because they are jealous of us. Jesus would not have wanted that."

The other young men cheered. "We need to fight."

One of the men raised his fists and yelled. "We've worked hard for what we have. Not just the land but all the manufacturing businesses and factories we own. Without us they have nothing. Czarina Catherine gave us all those privileges for a reason. And we kept our promise. We've made this country rich."

One of the older men stepped forward and shook his head. "Now come on, men! The new government won't throw us all out. The peasants have no idea how to farm and use all the machines we have brought to this country. Russia will fall apart. Why should the people work or study hard if there is no reason to do better? If everyone gets the same amount of favor and money? They'll just turn lazy. And somebody will take over and become a dictator. That's how it always works"

Finally, his face grim, the minister waved the men to silence. "This is not all about *things*. *About us*. No one has mentioned what worries me most. Marx did not believe in God. We are

Christians. I've talked to the people here. They say Lenin is like Marx and does not believe in God. I can't go along with that. Are we going to lose all our religious freedoms too? Will they burn our churches? Will we never be able to meet in groups and talk about God again?"

A middle-aged man called out, "People would never let that happen!"

The man sitting next to him waved his arm and grimaced. "No. No. Most of the people in Russia are Russian Orthodox. Even the peasants. And that is a Christian church too. And then there are many Muslims near where we lived. They believe in a God. They won't put up with that."

With great sadness in his voice, an elderly man, head bent, softly said, "We have lost all our land and animals already. We have nothing. Maybe we've been too privileged. Sometimes we forgot to treat the peasants who worked for us kindly, or as equals. You know, Franz is right. We are all children of God."

A young man next to Chnals shoved his desk away and jumped to his feet. "Are you saying we're to blame? That we are being punished by God?"

The old man's hands trembled. "Yes. Why should we always think we're the victims? We've done harm to others too."

The group suddenly silenced.

A few minutes later Mr. Talbert stepped forward and cleared his throat. "Klass speaks the truth. We must look at our part as well. There are always two sides to any issue. But now we need to get ready to leave and we all need to work together." He glanced around the room. "Has anyone here heard from their families in Ukraine recently?

No one answered. At last Papa rose. "No. We have no contact with Ukraine anymore since the Red Army destroyed everything.

We've had no mail for many months. We don't even know if our families are still alive."

Shocked, Chnals swallowed hard, and tried not to show his alarm. That meant that his grandparents had no idea what had happened to them, and didn't know they were coming. And Papa had no idea if his parents in Ukraine were still alive.

A murmur rose among the young men who sat together on one side of the group. The older men looked down or away.

The man with three children rose again. "Many of us have never even met our Ukrainian families. Why didn't anybody tell us?"

At last the minister stood up and said. "I know it's hard. We have no idea what we're facing. But we must trust that God will lead us."

The older men nodded, and the young men shook their heads in disgust.

Two days later, the families from the Tereker Settlement and many orphans, once again gathered at the train station. They carried only a couple of pillowcases packed with food and a few personal items.

Justina stared at Mama. "What happened to all our belongings we carried all the way from the Terek to Suworowka?"

Mama frowned and said nothing as she grabbed Maria just before she stumbled onto the train tracks.

Her voice tense and angry, Helena, still holding little Anchen in her arms muttered, "Those horrible soldiers! They stole everything! All we have is a few rubles that we strapped in pouches to our bodies or kept in our pockets all the time. Even while we slept."

Just then the conductor who had been hurrying from family group to family group, stopped next to Papa. The conductor frowned as Papa bargained with him for passage, but finally he asked, "How far are you going?"

Papa cleared his throat. "To Bakhmut. To stay with my parents." He pointed to Mama and the others. "This is my wife—and my children. We need a place to live," he said boldly.

The conductor checked the scanty crumpled pieces of paper money and shook his head. "You know that it's almost a thousand *werst*?"

Papa nodded and Mama, holding Maria, closed her eyes as though in prayer. Maria and Anchen both began to cry. Chnals kept studying the conductor's face for a sign. He frowned, then turned toward the children. At last the conductor took the rubles and waved his arm toward the train. The family, along with Otto and his sister, climbed into the cattle car.

Chnals glanced back at the people scrambling toward the cars. Mrs. Derksen! She waved at them and then turned away. Puzzled, he called to Mama. "Where's Mrs. Derksen going? I thought she was coming with us."

Mama rushed to the door and leaned forward out of the railroad car. Almost frantically she called to Mrs. Derksen. *"Auf wiedersehen*! *Auf wiedersehen*!"

And that was the last time the family saw or heard from Mrs. Derksen. She had come into their lives at a moment's notice to rescue them. And now, within a moment, she was gone.

STORY 18
Bakhmut, Ukraine

ANNA

THE PHONE RANG *and my dad stopped in mid sentence to answer it. As I expected, it was one of my aunties checking on us. It took forever! After about ten minutes I got up to retreat to my room, and prepare for school tomorrow. Dad turned around and called out, " Wait! I'm almost done here. Let's finish the story." Of course, I turned around, got some more hot tea, and sat down.*

CHNALS

Chnals sat down on a wooden bench and stared out the window, mesmerized by the chug, chug of the train on the tracks. He took a deep breath. How long had it been since they last rode the train from Chassow Jurt to Suworowka? He counted. Almost six months. It seemed like years ago. But this time there would be no army that would throw them off the train or try to kill them. The Red Army had moved south to Azerbaijan soon after they conquered southern Russia, and the White Army disintegrated and fled into the villages.

That night the train squealed to a stop and the conductor rushed through the railroad cars calling, "We are in Kuban. You have to get off. "

Papa rose to his feet. "What? Why? They told us we could go to Bakhmut without having to get off. We don't have any more rubles. You took them all!"

Without turning to Papa, the conductor called out as he ran through the car, "The Red Army needs the train. We can't say no to them."

A man behind them yelled, "That's crazy. What do they need it for? We've paid for this. Why can't they wait for the next train like everyone else?"

The conductor stopped and swung around. "They say they need the train to transport some of the soldiers and their equipment. They are still fighting in Ukraine."

Oh no! Ukraine? Would it ever end? Were his grandparents still alive? Maybe they'd have no place to live. Chnals bent forward and gritted his teeth.

The conductor called out again, "Hurry! Everybody. Get off!"

Quickly Chnals grasped Maria and swung her onto his shoulders. Papa grabbed Gerhard by the arms. Gerhard roused but seemed frozen in place. Helena picked up Anchen who lay on Mama's lap and cuddled her to her chest. Mama guided the other girls who each carried a pillow case filled with bread and a few dirty clothes, and followed Papa.

After two weeks of being thrown off the train in several villages and then boarding again on a later train, they finally neared Bakhmut. That morning, as the sun rose, Chnals woke up, still sitting in his seat. He bent his head toward the window and stared out onto the vast flat plains of Ukraine, the rich black chunks of tilled soil interrupting the miles and miles of ripe wheat fields and grass, swaying in the breeze. Everything seemed so peaceful. Maybe the fighting would be in other areas of Ukraine. He had to believe his grandparents were safe and would welcome their arrival.

When the train finally slowed and jerked to a stop, Chnals hurried off the train and took several deep breaths of clean air to clear his mind. Thank heaven all the villagers had shared their rubles and everyone had arrived to their destination. Several families had stayed by the Black Sea in Mariupol. Some had relocated to other trains heading east toward settlements by the Volga River.

He turned and saw Papa rush past him toward the train station, his face taut and stern. Oh no! What was going on? In his desperate need to catch a moment of sanity he had forgotten the rest of the family.

Then he rushed back to help his sisters and Gerhard onto the platform nearby.

Chnals turned to Mama who stood next to Helena with Anchen in her arms, sound asleep. "Where's Papa going?" Chnals whispered to Mama

"He's sending a wire to your grandparents so they'll know we're here." Her arms trembled and she tried to smile, but her eyes never wrinkled. He could feel her anxiety.

He tried to comfort her. "It'll be okay, Mama" he said, and placed his hand on her arm.

"Yes, yes," Mama said, standing up tall and clutching Anchen even tighter.

Chnals stepped back and studied the raggedy bunch huddled near the brick station. Miraculously they were still all healthy and together. He frowned. Would his grandparents have room for all of them? Twelve people, counting Otto and his sister?

That afternoon, Papa rented a wagon and horses from a nearby local farmer. After an hour of struggling and rumbling over the narrow dirt roads and bridges, the family arrived in the village of Alexanderpol, near Bakhmut, at Grandma and Grandpa Unger's house.

Papa jumped down off the wagon, not waiting for Mama, and ran to the front door of the modest brick farm house, surrounded by acres and acres of wheat and stubbled land. Mama handed Anchen to Helena. Then she pulled up her long, dark, blue skirt and climbed over the back of the wagon.

An older man and woman with graying hair that Chnals had never seen, opened the door and folded Mama and Papa into their arms. They must be Grandma and Grandpa Unger. Chnals sighed with relief. He could relax now. At last. This would be his new *home*.

A man about Papa's age and four young children, probably from age three to age ten, peered out of the door behind his grandparents. Who were they? Papa shook the man's hand, and they stood and talked for a minute. He heard Mama's voice shake as she hugged the man, but he couldn't hear what they said.

At last Papa turned around and called from the front porch, "Come, come, children. Meet your grandparents. And your Uncle Henry." Chnals hesitated. His uncle? Then the children must be his cousins. Where was their mother?

His brother and sisters climbed over the back wagon wheel and dashed toward the porch. Otto and his sister hesitated, then followed slowly behind them. "Me! Me!" three year old Maria cried out. She looked squarely at Chnals, but pointed to the grass. "Me down." Finally he grabbed her and swung her over his shoulders, then balanced her on his back as he scrambled over the side of the four-wheeled wagon. With Maria still on his back, he held on to her small hands and strode toward Papa.

With a giant smile Grandma Unger gently pulled Maria from Chnals's shoulder and held her close. "My, what a beautiful girl you are, Maria. Are you hungry?"

Three year old Maria looked up into Grandma Unger's face as though measuring her smile to make sure it was safe, and then said, "Persky."

Grandma burst out laughing. "Well, not today, but we have sugar cookies."

Maria smacked her lips and clapped her hands.

As they entered the front door Chnals took a deep breath and his whole body lit up. He felt his tummy roll and growl. Roast beef! His mouth began to water. By now he had almost forgotten roast beef even existed. And then his mind raced back to the Tereker Settlement. A year ago roast beef had been an ordinary and frequent dinner cooked by his mother. He had never imagined there would come a time in his life when he and his family would run for their lives and almost starve.

Grandma Unger called out. "Come in and sit down. Dinner is ready." Chnals walked into the dining room behind his sisters and noticed Grandma had set up two large wooden tables for the group. She ushered the younger children to one of the tables. Then she pointed to the other one. All the adults seemed to know this table was meant for them. Puzzled, Chnals checked the number of settings. The children's table was full. Where was he supposed to sit?

Mama motioned to Chnals and Helena. "You two come here and sit with us. You're adults now."

After Grandpa said a long prayer of thanksgiving for their safety, everyone waited for Grandma and Mama to serve the food. As Chnals had been taught, only the adults were allowed to speak during meals. And even then, sparingly. The children remained quiet. After they finished a delicious dinner of roast beef, green beans, and boiled potatoes with real gravy, Helena jumped up and hurried to help Mama and Grandma clear the table and wash the dishes.

The younger children grabbed a couple of balls and ran out to play in the back yard. Mama motioned to Sara and Justina. "You go out with the children and make sure they're okay." They nodded and hurried out the back door.

Chnals could hear the excited chatter of the children as they rushed about creating new rules for their game. He wanted to join them but turned away from the door and scolded himself. He had better things to do now that he was an adult, though he had no idea what that would be. He stood at the kitchen door and watched the men, wondering what he should do next. That way he could see both the kitchen and the dining room. This being an adult was entirely new to him. And he wasn't sure he liked it.

He heard an anxious whisper come from his mother as she leaned over to Grandma, in the kitchen, "Has anyone here seen or heard from my parents?"

Grandma Unger looked down and shook her head slowly. "No. I'm sorry. We thought they would be with you. We have heard nothing."

He saw his mother heave a deep sigh and her hands shake as she wiped the cutlery. "We have no idea what happened to them. We think they escaped after we did from Village #9, but we don't even know that."

A moment later Papa motioned to Chnals. "Come. Come sit with us." The men gathered in the living room and sat down on the plush brown sofa and upholstered chairs scattered about in a circle.

Papa leaned toward Uncle Henry and Grandpa. "It sounds quiet here in the neighborhood. Is the Red Army still fighting here or have they left?"

Grandpa leaned back. "They have mostly left Ukraine."

The group of men sat in silence for a few minutes, and then Papa pulled his chair closer to Uncle Henry. "I'm so sorry about Marta. She was a good woman. How did it happen?"

Uncle Henry slid forward on the sofa. His voice faltered. "The Peasants here are turning into bandits. They hate us because we have money and own land. I shouldn't have gone. But I went to help Marta's parents bring in the wheat crop. Marta stayed home with the children. Our neighbors saw some of the bandits ride up to our house. Marta must have hidden the children and tried to keep the men from coming in. She had piled furniture in front of the door, but they broke the windows and shot her. They stole everything that was worth anything." He hesitated and wiped away tears. Then he held his head high and struggled to continue.

"It's okay, Henry," Papa said quietly. "You don't need to go on. We'll talk about it some other day."

No, no," Uncle Henry said. "I want to tell you. They lit the house on fire. We were so lucky the neighbors saw what happened. They rushed into the burning building and grabbed the children and Marta's body. They brought them all to their house. We buried Marta in the meadow behind our house when I got home. Everything we owned is gone."

Chnals shuddered. His mind grasped onto the images and the feelings still whirling in his Uncle Henry's head. The horror and pain he must have felt when he arrived home to a dead wife and a burnt house! But also the joy and gratitude he had felt when he found his children alive at the neighbors.

"I never met Marta, but from everything your parents have written to us, she was a wonderful wife and mother. I'm so sorry. This should never have happened," Mama said, a hint of anger in her voice.

Chnals whirled around. Mama? Mama and Grandma Unger stood at the door listening. Mama held a dish of sugar cookies. She placed them on a wooden hand crafted center table and sat down next to Papa.

Grandma Unger addressed the group. "I'm afraid we're all pretty tired. It's been a long day. We need to figure out where everybody is going to sleep." She looked up at Papa. "Henry has four young children, and you have ten with Otto and his sister."

Grandpa frowned and sat very still for a few minutes, then said, "I have an idea. We have a big attic and we'll separate the girls and boys with a hanging blanket."

Chnals gritted his teeth and blinked. Sleep with all those girls up there? No way! At last he decided to check the attic for himself. Maybe it wouldn't be so bad if they could make the attic into two rooms. If he helped, he could choose where he slept. He stood up and said, "Can I help?"

"Yes. We need everyone to help." Grandpa Unger beckoned to him with his arm just like Papa always did. "The adults and the youngest children will sleep downstairs. The rest of you will sleep upstairs. Henry, you get the rope and take it to the attic."

Grandma hurried to the small sewing room near the living room, and began to pile knitted and crocheted wool blankets, as well as quilts, into the hall. Grandpa, Papa, and Chnals each gathered some of the blankets and climbed up the rather rickety, steep, wooden stairs near the front door. The attic had only one window, but the sun shone brightly and lit up the giant room.

A few minutes later Uncle Henry appeared with several ropes. He unfurled them and tied them together, then attached the now long rope to the beam in the middle of the attic. Grandpa hung a couple of outside farm blankets he had used to cover the horses, on the rope to divide the attic.

Chnals separated the quilts and knitted blankets, and dumped them into the two rooms. Each of the kids would select one blanket at bed time and snuggle into their chosen spot. He grabbed a plain woolen quilt for himself and placed it near the window. Looking out the window, he half expected Mount Elbrus to jut out into the sky to welcome him home. No. He swallowed hard. He would never see his mountain again. This would never be home.

The stairs creaked and Papa ran to the entry way. What was going on? Then Chnals saw Grandma's head poke up into the attic.

"Mama! What are you doing?" Papa called out to her.

Panting, she pulled herself up on the rough wooden floor. "Here," she said, handing Papa a large box. "This old attic needs something to make it more cheery for the children." She hauled out Christmas ornaments, pictures, toys, and cookies, turned the box upside down and placed the items on top of it. "Chnals, you help the others put up the decorations when they come in."

Chnals nodded. "Yes, I will Grandma." He bowed slightly to her.

"Don't let them eat all the cookies at once." She laughed and hid some of the cookies inside the wooden box. "This will have to do as a table."

That evening, when Chnals and the other children crawled up the stairs to go to bed, he noticed that Papa had roped off a small room in the middle of the attic, and added a bucket and some paper. Chnals gasped. A toilet! There was no way he'd use it. He thought for a minute, then decided if he needed to, he would sneak out and go hide in the trees behind the house so no one would see him. His sisters had teased him and Gerhard when they were younger about how lucky they were to be boys.

At last he settled down on his blanket on the floor and checked the window. No Mount Elbrus! But the moon! The moon, now almost full, shone brightly over the dark prairie land to welcome him. He took a deep breath and his whole body relaxed. Yes, the moon had followed them, had protected them, and served them everywhere they had run to hide. "Thank you, God," he whispered.

ANNA

Our giant grandfather clock struck ten times, and Dad stopped talking. He stared out the dark window of the living room into nothing, just as Grandpa had so many times. Pain flooded his face. I waited. Then waited some more.

At last he looked back at me and stood up. In a gruff voice he said, "It's time for bed. We need to leave early tomorrow to get you back to school."

By this time I knew what he was doing. He couldn't finish the story because the memories had overwhelmed him one more time. But this night I refused to let him leave. I jumped up and in a stern voice I said, "Dad, you promised me!"

I expected him to yell at me as he had so many times in the past. Instead tears came to his eyes, and his body began to shake. He sat back down and took my hand. "Yes. You're right. What would you like to know?"

"What happened after you got to Bakhmut?"

Dad leaned back and seemed deep in thought. At last he said, "I've told you about the Red Army and the White Army in Russia, But right after we came to my grandparents place there was a Black Army as well."

Puzzled I blurted out, "A Black Army?" *I had never heard of them.* "Why did they pick all these colors? Red, White, and Black?"

Dad smiled. "They called themselves the Black Army because they were all poor, Ukrainian, anarchist peasants. Their leader was called Makhno. He hated the German people. He had to work for us in the past to make enough money to survive. The German people were rich and his family was very poor. It was the Black Army that burned my uncle's house and killed my aunt. That would be your great-uncle and -aunt."

"Oh my gosh, Dad. I'm so sorry."

"My uncle and my four cousins had nowhere to live, so they moved in with my grandparents. But we had no idea what was going on. And then we came too. Mom and Dad and ten extra children. After a little while, another family took in Otto and his sister. We lived this way for five years. Sixteen people. And then your Aunt Betty was born during the famine in 1921." *He shook his head and his voice faltered.* "You still have several relatives who live in Russia."

I blinked hard and sat up straight, staring at my dad. "Are you telling me I still have relatives in Russia and Ukraine?"

He nodded. "Yes. Most of them were sent to Siberia. The men had to work in the mines. We have never been able to find out what happened to them since the Communist government took over."

"*Do you know what happened to your Oma and Opa Schmidt? Did they survive?*"

Dad took a huge breath. "*Like I said, when we arrived in Bakhmut, no one knew where they were, or if they were still alive.*" Then a large smile transformed his face. "*But here is one of those amazing miracles we experienced during that time. Oma and Opa left to the south of the Tereker villages with several other families from Village #9. A year after we arrived at Grandpa and Grandma Unger's house, they turned up in Bakhmut where they had lived before they moved to the Tereker Settlement.*"

"*Wow! Really?*" I said. I wanted to jump up and hug my dad, but that's not what good German girls did in those days. I could only imagine what my grandmother must have felt when they suddenly appeared. Yes, what a miracle. I wanted to cry with her and shout for joy. But she died of a heart attack only ten years after they arrived in Canada, even before I was born." *Did they escape to Canada with you?*" I asked.

Dad shook his head. "*No, they didn't want to go. They were tired of running and hiding. We had to leave them and my grandparents Unger behind. After we left, we never saw any of our grandparents or most of our extended family again. Just two of my uncles from Oma's side, the Schmidt side, escaped to Canada a few years later. You've met them. They live in Ontario.*"

I couldn't remember meeting them, but I said nothing.

"*We had no idea what was going on in Ukraine when we arrived,*" Dad continued. "*We thought we'd be safe.*" He hesitated for a while, then his shoulders collapsed. Voice trembling, he looked straight into my eyes. "*Anna, you need to know . . . war . . . war is unspeakable horror. I don't understand why people keep thinking we can solve our problems that way. It doesn't work. It never has. And it never will.*" He stared out the window into the darkness *again in silence. Then he suddenly rose from his chair and hurried to his bedroom.*

After that long weekend, the stories ended. From then on, whenever I asked my dad or my aunties about their experiences in Ukraine from 1918-1924, they looked away and changed the subject. It was only much later, when I listened to several other people who had escaped with Dad's family from Ukraine that I pieced together what happened.

STORY 19
Ukraine at War: The Black Army

September 1918 – July 1924

LIKE SO MANY other refugees and veterans of war, my father and his family did not speak about the horrendous years of war in Ukraine, except for brief references to particular events. I had no idea what happened after Dad's family settled in at Grandma and Grandpa Unger's house in Bakhmut. But I always wondered. It was as though their lives suddenly came to a halt and *poofed* into nothingness for the next five years. And then they left Ukraine and Russia and miraculously appeared in Canada in August of 1924, exactly a hundred years ago now.

Sometimes when my parents invited Dad's friends who had also escaped Russia, Dad and the men grabbed the old decorative oak chairs from around the dining room table and carried them into Mom and Dad's bedroom while the women and children sat in the living room visiting and playing games, drinking juice or tea. Then I'd hear a click and I knew Dad had locked the door. When I'd ask Mom what the men were doing, she would lift her shoulders, scowl, shake her head, and return to her conversation with the other women.

It was not until years later, speaking to some other refugees from Ukraine who had survived the Russian Revolution and were now also living in Winnipeg, that I finally discovered the truth. At least, the truth as they saw it. I learned of the intense fear that each of the refugees felt because they had not left Russia legally. According to them several men had been killed by poison or captured and placed in Russian prisons. Why? Because "they knew too much." No one mentioned what *they* knew. That remained the secret spoken only behind the locked door of my parents' bedroom.

In the early 1970s, my husband, Ron, a research scientist for the USDA, corresponded regularly about scientific information with a Ukrainian-Russian scientist in Kyiv, USSR. Even though the Russian government opened all their letters, they forged a unique and close friendship. Larry wanted us to come for a conference in Moscow, and to visit his family. We decided to go, especially because we could see friends in Europe at the same time.

When I told Dad about the trip, I thought he'd be excited. Instead, he began to shake and buckled onto a nearby chair. He started pleading with us. "Please, please children . . . please, please don't go. We didn't leave legally. They will take your passport, Anna, and will never let you come back. We'll never see you again."

I gasped. That man who I thought to always be strong suddenly disintegrated right before my eyes. Ron and I disappeared to the front porch of my parents' new home in the town where I had gone to high school.

Ron put his arm around me and whispered, "I'm so sorry. I didn't know. This is the kind of torture refugees like your dad go through every day. We can't make it worse for him. We won't go."

I leaned into him, closed my eyes, and gently nodded. "You're right. We can't go."

To honor my father's wishes, I have never visited Ukraine or Russia. At the time, I thought my dad had an exaggerated fear of Stalin and Russia, but after all we have experienced at this point with Putin, a former KGB agent, and the death of Alexei Navalny, I no longer doubt him.

Over the years, listening to other refugees who had escaped Ukraine after the revolution, and reading up on history, I was finally able to place the last pieces of the puzzle together. Just around the time my dad's family arrived in Bakhmut in 1918, an impoverished and angry peasant man, Nestor Makhno, formed the anarchist Black Army of disenfranchised and often desperately poor peasants. Makhno and other peasants had worked on the farms and factories of German landlords whom he felt had mistreated him and other peasant servants.

Makhno and his men wished to create a stateless and classless society, an Anarchist Free Territory. His people called it anarcho-communism. They hated all the wealthy landowners they had served, and wanted to seize their land, divide it, and distribute it to the peasants. The revolution became their avenue for revenge. They also called for freedom of speech, press, assembly, and unions. To reach this goal, the Black Army allied with the Red Army, but refused to merge with them.

Although my dad never spoke about Makhno, my uncle and his friends did. They talked about how much the peasants envied the Germans for all the rights Catherine the Great had bestowed on the German people that they, as Russians, had never received. Makhno, as well as other peasants, had struggled to survive by working for wealthy German landlords. These landowners were called Kulaks and the German people were considered among this group.

As I searched for more puzzle pieces, I turned to encyclopedias as well as writings in German, recorded by survivors. Then it finally made even more sense.

In 1914, at the outbreak of World War I, Russia joined Britain and other allies (eventually including the USA) to fight the Germans. However, when the German soldiers invaded Ukraine, they automatically gravitated to the German people living there, who in turn befriended the soldiers.

In 1917, when the Bolshevik Communist Party seized power of the capital of Russia, Lenin decided to withdraw Russia from World War I. The civil war officially began. Soon after, all the German soldiers left the country. Many young soldiers had fallen for German-Russian women and married them. They took them to Germany.

Although the German-Russian people never gave formal assistance to the German army, they were perceived as traitors by the Russians (maybe a little like some in America viewed the Japanese immigrants during World War II).

Every day the Black Army grew in number and ferocity. Fueled by this final perceived betrayal, on top of their existing resentments, men raced through the German villages on horseback and snatched women. They gang-raped young women, even mothers and children, and killed them. Often they forced the men to watch. In one household the bandits shot everyone in the family, young and old, cut off their heads, and arranged them on the dining room table. Sometimes they poisoned the children.

Many small German villages, close to where my dad's family lived, were entirely destroyed, burned, looted, and most of the people murdered. Thousands of people were killed and left on the land, mostly unburied. The Black Army stole all their valuables, as well as their crops and animals, especially the horses. Total fear and anarchy followed.

In early 1919, only months after my family arrived in Bakhmut, the German men, especially the young ones, (as young as the early teens) formed their own army called the *Selbstschutz* (the self-protection army). They stationed several young men at lookouts in different villages. If they saw Makhno's army in the distance coming towards them, they hid all the women and children in underground cellars, and chased off the Black Army, guns blazing.

Was my dad a part of the *Selbstschutz*? He never spoke of it. I had never seen Dad use a rifle. But then I found out Dad was a perfect shot with his rifle when he killed, with one bullet, a skunk that decided to take residence in the chicken barn. One day when I was watching the news, I expressed anger at how the soldiers were treating some of the people on the battlefield. My father shook his head and leaned over to me. "Anna, you have no idea what you would do if you were placed into that situation." Those words have stayed with me to this day.

By late 1919 and early 1920, the Red Army again captured Eastern and Central Ukraine and defeated Nestor Makhno. In October, 1920, the Bolsheviks signed an armistice with Poland, and the Red Army took over Ukraine. The Russian revolution finally ended in 1923 when the Communist Red Army, headed by Lenin, overcame both the Black Army and the White Army. Nestor Makhno, exiled from Ukraine, fled to Romania.

The Communists under Lenin confiscated the land, food, and animals from Ukraine, and the bread basket of Russia that the German immigrants had worked so hard to create, collapsed. With the economy in shambles, and all the technological factories the German people had built to create mechanical equipment destroyed, many of the people were tossed off their land. All of the animals had been stolen or killed. The Red Army burned or took all the crops to feed the army.

Shortly after, a drought swept the land. The great famine of 1921 – 1922 destroyed the country and its population. No land, no crops, no animals. Many, many people lost their homes and their lives. According to statistics found in Wikipedia, five to eight million people died of starvation. Thirty million were considered malnourished. They resorted to eating crows, potato peels, and bread when available, or made soup from weeds. Both America and Canada sent shiploads of food when the Russian government finally allowed it.

My Aunt Helena sometimes talked of standing in line for food, so starved that she felt she would not be able to lift a sack of potatoes and carry it home. She knew all the rest of the family would be waiting at the gate to run the sack over to Mama to finally cook something besides bread for dinner. I never saw a meal at my grandfather's farm without potatoes. Throughout their marriage, Dad demanded Mom cook potatoes for dinner, and often fry potatoes for breakfast or supper as well.

According to my aunties, Grandma baked bread every day with wheat from their hidden underground stash. And each day starving people circled their house, begging for food. With tears running down her cheeks, Grandma tore pieces of bread from a loaf and handed them through their wooden fence to starving, wasting children.

And then one day in 1921, a tiny little baby was born: my Aunt Elizabetha, the amazing miracle who survived one of the worst recorded famines on earth. She lived to be seventy-two years old. Although she grew to be only a skinny 4'10" tall, she was the feistiest of the aunties, who always wore three-inch spike-heeled shoes. And kicked out every obstacle in her path.

I used to wonder why my dad would get so upset at my mom if there was no meat on the table for meals. So I asked him one time when I was around eleven or twelve. His answer was simple. "I will never go without meat in my life again."

Of course, innocent little me, said, "Why not? You know nutritionists say, people don't need meat every day."

My dad turned and stared out the window, as he had so often before, and I knew his mind was far, far, away in Russia. At last he said, "Those years of famine when we lived in Ukraine with your great-grandparents, we had no meat. Sometimes your grandpa would buy meat in the village, but then we stopped."

"Why?" I asked. That seemed irrational.

Dad hesitated and without looking at me, he finally said in a quiet, faraway voice, "We had no idea what kind of meat we were eating." That made sense to me. During a famine, I could see that people might kill and eat their dogs and cats to survive. I nodded my head. He never elaborated.

It was not until years later, while doing some research about that era in Russia, that I finally realized what my dad had meant. I gasped and my jaw dropped. Cannibalism! Common in that famine, the books stated. I closed my eyes and my stomach did a quick flip. I wondered. *Would I eat other humans to survive?* I assumed the people who sold human meat in Ukraine had found bodies of individuals who had starved to death, then butchered them to cook, eat, and sell. It was just like the stories of the Donner Party I had read.

Of course. Survival. Our deepest instinct.

In 1922 the communist party finally signed a treaty between Russia, Ukraine, and other eastern European countries they had conquered, to form the Union of Soviet Socialist Republic (USSR). No religions were allowed. Instead of believing in God they believed in the State.

I remember one day when I snuck into the living room and heard my Aunt Helena speak to her friends about those days in communist Russia when she started school in Ukraine. Each day the students stood up tall and repeated a new pledge to the USSR. They vowed to conquer the whole world and spread communism, one country at a time. All semblances of free speech and religion disappeared.

A friend of hers asked, "Is it true that Communists don't believe in God?"

My aunt nodded. Her voice broke as she said, "If we wanted to continue our education after elementary school, or needed a job, they made us sign a contract swearing that we did not believe in God. But how could we do that? It would be a lie and God would know we had denied Him. Many people refused and they suffered." I wanted to know what happened to the people who refused, but I dared not come into the room and show I had listened.

Later, I read that all the churches had been destroyed. If people gathered for worship or spoke against Communism, they were severely punished, beaten, or imprisoned. Several of Dad's relatives were sent to Siberia to work in the mines. People spied and told on their neighbors, friends, and family members in order to gain favors from the government, or to secure their and their family's lives. The villagers lived each day in complete silence about their beliefs in God, and their thoughts about the government. But many still gathered in small groups hidden away, fearful, always in different homes, to worship God and speak freely, praying they would not be discovered.

I knew so little about war and its consequences when I was fourteen, living in Canada. It was merely a concept out there in the great open prairie, somewhere far away. All I remember about the Korean War as a child was seeing my dad, huddled over the radio after dinner, listening to the evening news on the Canadian Broadcasting Corporation. He gritted his teeth and clutched his hands on the desk where the radio sat. He would bark at us if we disturbed him. "*Shh*.. Not now!"

At the time I had very little idea why he seemed so afraid. But each day we said a prayer for the soldiers and the innocent people in Korea before we went to bed. "God, please end the war and don't let it spread." I thought my dad was merely fearful of what had happened at the end of World War II. The atomic bomb. As schoolchildren, we didn't hide under desks like Americans did, and we were not particularly concerned. We thought Russia would bomb America, not Canada. After all, we didn't have anything the Russians wanted

STORY 20

Escape

IN JANUARY, 1924, Lenin died and Stalin took his place. And from everything my family said, Stalin quickly became a dictator, took all their land, killing massive numbers of his own people if they did not obey him or were disloyal. For the German people, the land they had considered paradise in the 1700s and 1800s, had turned into a living hell.

At this time many of the German people escaped the country. In July, 1924, my grandparents along with the entire nuclear family of nine children, from ages three to twenty-one, once again paid many rubles to the conductor of a local train and hid under blankets in cattle cars, in complete silence. My dad had just turned eighteen.

Leaving everything behind, including all their relatives and friends, they boarded a train to Latvia in the middle of the night. My grandfather and Dad spoke of the incredible relief and joy they all felt as they crossed the border into Latvia without being discovered. The children threw off their blankets and began to jump up and down and sing.

Shortly after they arrived in Riga, a man came to escort them to a small British ship docked in the harbor, waiting for refugees from Russia. They sailed to South Hampton and then to Liverpool, England. A couple of weeks later, they boarded the hull of a large ship, *Montclare,* to Canada.

I'll never forget a family gathering only a few years before my father died at eighty-eight of Parkinson's disease. He was already ill, but on one of Ron and my visits, the family gathered at the aunties for dinner. It was "memory lane" time, and the aunties all raved about what a wonderful time they had on the trip across the Atlantic Ocean to Quebec in 1924.

My dad, in his usual Sunday dark suit, white shirt, and blue tie, shook his head and muttered. "What are you talking about? Three weeks of hell! Hundreds of people in steerage with no real toilets and no water to wash up. The British fed us. That was great. But the storms were so bad that everyone threw up all over the place. And the lice!"

Aunt Jessie burst into laughter. "Yes, yes, Chnals," she said. "And you used to abandon us and go help the sailors on deck. They loved you. The storms were so awful that Mom and Dad were scared you would be blown overboard."

Dad nodded his head, grinned, and hunched forward in his wheelchair. "Ah yes….I see you girls figured it out, didn't you? I couldn't handle the horrible stench. Besides, I was eighteen and I needed something to do. I didn't speak a word of English, but that didn't matter. It was a good thing I had learned a kind of sign language to communicate with the Muslim boys when I was just twelve."

Aunt Teena touched his shoulder and gave him a hug. "You know, we never noticed the smell. We were just so excited to be free. We could say anything and do anything without being scared someone would tell on us or kill us." She turned to address us. "Do you have any idea what it's like to be so scared all the time that we'd say something or do something wrong, and the whole family could go to prison or be killed?"

I did an internal gasp. Wow! No wonder my father kept repeating, "Never, never let your freedoms go."

Aunt Anne in her usual jovial way changed the subject. "I was only five, but I remember every day those three weeks on the ocean. Even though we didn't speak any English, we would jump around and play with the other kids on the ship. We had so much fun! More fun than we had had since I was born. You have no idea how happy and thankful I am that we escaped Russia and came to Canada."

All the aunties nodded.

On August 8, 1924, the ship finally arrived in Montreal, Quebec. From there the refugees were sent by rail to Ottawa, Ontario, the capital of Canada. A man from the Department of Immigration strode into their railroad car to greet them and sort out where they would be settling. The man asked several questions in German. Then he simply asked, "Do you have any relatives in Canada?"

"Yes," my grandfather said without hesitation. "My wife has an aunt here."

"Where exactly does she live?" he asked.

Tired and annoyed by now, Grandpa raised his voice. "In Canada!"

The man scowled, shook his head, and shrugged. "That doesn't help us much. Canada is a very large country. Like Russia."

Grandpa gritted his teeth and looked away.

At last the man added, "You were farmers in Ukraine, right? Canada very much needs farmers. We'll put you on the train to go west."

Grandpa smiled and nodded. "We can settle down anywhere we have good land and water to grow wheat."

Even though she was only three years old at the time, my Aunt Betty (Elizabetha), with pride in her voice, often told the story of disembarking from the train and seeing an elderly woman on the street, selling cookies. Grandpa strode to the woman and said, "I want a cookie for my little girl." He handed her the last few pennies he had left. And Aunt Betty got her cookie!

A few days later, the family boarded the cross-country train, the Canadian Pacific Railway. They sped across Ontario and stopped west of Winnipeg, Manitoba. Grandpa always glowed as he spoke of seeing the dark, rich soil of the Canadian prairie. "Just like our home, Ukraine" he would say. Even then, Ukraine was well known as one of the most fertile lands on the planet.

And then, the miracle that my family most often spoke of happened. As the train stopped at the station, a young man who spoke German, jumped onto the train and entered their car to help them find a place to stay.

The young man asked. "Do you have any relatives here?"

Poor Grandpa hesitated as though afraid to give the wrong answer. At last he said, "We have an aunt in Canada."

"Oh really? Do you know where she lives?" the young man asked.

Grandpa shook his head. "No. We don't know."

The young man looked puzzled. "What is her name?"

Grandma stepped forward, still holding Elizabetha in her arms. "Her name is Katherine Schmidt."

The young man gasped and turned white. "I think that might be my mother-in-law," he whispered. And sure enough. It was Dad's great-aunt Katherine who had left Russia several years ago.

The next day the young man took the entire family with their two boxes of treasured goods from Russia to stay at Aunt Katherine's house in Winkler. Grandpa, Dad, and Helena worked for Mrs. Schmidt and other families on nearby farms, cleaning, and harvesting crops, until they had enough money to rent a large brick house in the neighborhood, shared with another family. All the younger children attended public school.

About two years later, they finally moved to the Steinbach area, southeast of Winnipeg, where they bought a farm of their own. All the older children were required to work and contribute most of their money to pay for the *Reiseschultz* (travel debt), and the farm. None of the kids were allowed to leave home or marry. My parents dated for three years before the debt was paid. They finally married in 1934 and, with the help of Mom's parents, who were fairly wealthy, bought a large farm of their own. It remained a lucrative business for them until they retired forty years later. At that time my parents bought three homes in town with the proceeds from the farm, and rented them out to other families.

Throughout their lives, much of my parent's savings were donated to help the poor. During the Vietnam War, my aunties and family took in and mentored an entire refugee family of husband and wife with five children from Cambodia. The parents immediately procured jobs "plucking chickens" at a nearby meat factory, and the children attended public school. Years later I learned that the entire refugee family had moved to Winnipeg to live, study, and work. The children had all received their degrees at the University of Manitoba, and now were married with well-paying jobs in the area. I guess today we would say, "My family paid it forward."

All of Dad's family, except Grandma, lived to be in their seventies and eighties. My Aunt Anne, an incredible, resilient, woman, born during their flight from the Tereker Settlement to Ukraine, always laughing and helping others, lived to be one hundred years old.

I have no idea how, but in 1976 Dad discovered one of his cousin's address in Russia and sent her a letter. She was elated and wrote back immediately and included a picture. Unbelievable!

Fifty-two years since they had seen each other. Dad had always assumed all his family in Russia had died. He corresponded with three of his cousins from Bakhmut, Ukraine until 1989. Then in 1990, after the collapse of the Soviet Union, one of dad's cousins, with her entire family, immigrated to Germany. She and Dad continued writing letters until 1993. I still have those letters, both from Russia and from Germany. Recently I translated them from German into English.

I laughed when his cousin asked if he still spoke Russian. My Dad, speak Russian? Never! I didn't even know he knew the language. Although I'm not sure, I believe he felt he'd be a traitor to Canada if he spoke Russian. All the letters I still have are bland with nothing negative about the government, or about their beliefs in God.

My husband pointed out, "Of course. The communists opened all their letters both ways and read them. They had to be careful. Who would know better than your dad not to do something stupid and endanger his cousins?"

Dad often shook his head as he watched TV during the collapse of Communism. "This is not the end. You are kidding yourself if you believe that." Although my dad died in 1995, before Putin came to power in Russia, I could almost see him now shake his head, tears filling his eyes, saying, "KGB. I told you. It isn't over. They want the world and they will do anything to get it."

And I see, exactly a hundred years since my family's escape from Russia, the identical toll war is taking again on the innocent people of Ukraine—the mothers, the fathers, and especially the children. Bakhmut is now again under Russian control.

Ukrainians, please know, my father would be proud of you. "Be strong," were his favorite words. "Never, never let your freedoms go."

REFLECTIONS

LIKE SO MANY refugees, my father, my uncle, and his oldest two sisters had all the signs and symptoms of Post Traumatic Stress Disorder (PTSD). But it was not until I studied psychology in college, and then became a psychotherapist, that I understood my dad. Interestingly, most of the studies I read, never mentioned how the children of refugees were affected by their parents experiences.

In the early developmental stages of childhood, I as most children, believed that my dad's explosions were my fault. If only I could figure out what I had done wrong, I could make it all stop. I spent hours, days, months, years trying to change my behavior. But nothing worked. Obviously I wasn't smart enough. I wasn't good enough. One time I would say or do something to please him, and he would smile and pat me on the shoulder, and the next time I would do the same thing, and he would fly into a rage.

Sometimes when Dad began to talk about their terrifying experiences in Ukraine, his face flushed, his voice rose, and he began to tremble. I remember I would hold my breath and stand very still. When my mom was around, she would rush forward and say, "Chnals, don't talk about that. It just makes it worse."

There were times I heard him scream in the middle of the night, and heard him pace the hall. Sometimes he jumped up for what seemed no reason and ran out of the house, then would not speak to us for hours. Occasionally he would yell, explode, and throw things, but I never knew why.

Often when Dad came home from the fields and I could tell he was anxious, I would hide in my bedroom or out in one of our barns with the animals. I dreaded the winters because he spent more time at home with us. I certainly understood the old saying, "walking on egg shells."

When Dad was home we worked. We were not allowed to laugh and play. Although I felt much too young to leave home to go to high school on my own at 14, I also felt relief.

When I read about the many veterans of war disappearing into the wilderness by themselves for months at a time, I understood why Dad spent so many, many, hours by himself, working the land and taking care of the animals. I used to think he was merely a loner who rarely smiled or laughed, until my aunties told stories about how many friends Dad had before the war, and how he loved to laugh and play.

The reason he stopped at the most vital places in the stories he told me, had nothing to do with trying to keep me in suspense. As I got older, I could often tell when he was reliving the war. He would swallow hard and look far, far away just like my grandpa had.

A few months before my high school graduation, my sister presented me with a train ticket to Vancouver, British Columbia. We would travel together. What an amazing gift! Lee and I were so excited we danced around and chattered making endless plans. I noticed Dad pace up and down in the living room, clenching his jaw. Finally Dad burst out, "Girls, you have no idea what will happen, We may all be dead by then." The future to him was a total unknown. Now I understand. His family dropped their entire lives, everything, and fled in less than twenty-four hours.

In those days I looked at my mom to help me understand Dad's fears, but she frowned and turned away. My parents, as many others, did not communicate with us about feelings. My sister learned to close her ears and pretend nothing happened. I, on the other hand, heard, saw, and felt everything. I often wished I could be more like Lee.

At Ron and my wedding, we played around, laughing and being silly. He sat down on the ground and I jumped into his lap. All my friends cheered and took pictures, but Dad stomped forward and said in a gruff voice, "Stop that! Getting married is serious business." I shrank into myself and felt like a little child again. I was doing it wrong. Whatever *it* was. On retrospect, I realize one of the reasons I fell in love with Ron was that he was a brilliant scientist, but most of all that he loved to laugh and play.

Sometimes people ask, "Are you saying four of your aunties never married?" In those days I used to wonder why also. They were beautiful women, gregarious and loved to have fun, not like my dad! It was not until much later that I realized how afraid they were of men, especially strangers. I can only guess, but my oldest aunty, my Aunt Helena, dipped down into deep depressions at times and hid from people. Although she never spoke of it, it was obvious to me, she had been raped.

I'm sure you've heard the saying "Like peas in a pod." The four of them were four peas in a pod. If anyone tried to peel the shell away and strip them apart, they would hold on so tight no one could break the armor. All the way to their death. According to my mom, my Aunt Anne was engaged when she was young, but cancelled the wedding at the last minute.

Although the aunts and uncles showed few emotions, they always hugged, kissed and said a prayer for protection when people left. It seemed as though they were afraid that they would never see each other again.

While in his fifties, Dad had surgery to replace one of his ear drums. The doctor noticed his shaking hands and agitated manner, and asked him what was going on. My dad did not answer. According to my mother, the doctor asked him a simple question, "War?" And Dad nodded. The doctor handed him a prescription for Valium. That little white pill felt like a miracle, both to him and our family. Fortunately he never abused the drug.

Recently one of my friends who had read a few of my stories said, "Your dad sounds like a really good man." My answer was, "Yes, a very good man. *And* he had PTSD—Like so many good people who have faced death day in and day out, as they run for their lives,"

Under life threatening conditions, in order to save themselves or someone else, humans react first with their amygdala, the emotional brain, before the prefrontal cortex, the cognitive brain steps in. Usually we think before we feel and make a decision to act, but in this case, we feel before we think and act. Dad, as many other people who have experienced severe trauma, did not have control over his life at that moment of memory. With the study of epigenetics, we now know that even the children of people with PTSD can inherit symptoms and vulnerabilities for up to 3 generations.

When I flew to Winnipeg to see him in September, 1995, just before he died of Parkinsons disease, there was a sudden switch in his demeanor while my sister fed him pudding in his wheelchair. I don't quite know how to explain it, but he suddenly turned to me. He appeared completely lucid and present. He smiled and looked deep into my eyes, Then he whispered, "Forgive me." He did not say what I should forgive him for. I placed his trembling hand in mine and looked back into his eyes. "I forgive you Dad. Please forgive me if I have hurt you."

He nodded slightly, closed his eyes, and slid back into near unconsciousness. He died a week later.

Although the family trauma influenced me in several negative ways, I also learned to be more resilient and to have deep empathy for others. I guess what we take away from our experiences is our choice. What I learned from my dad has stayed with me all my life.

So often I heard Dad repeat the following words:

"Anna, always be strong. Be strong."

"Be afraid but do it anyway."

"Always keep your promise. If you don't, people won't trust you, and you will hurt them."

"Work hard. Be responsible. Become educated."

"Help others in need. It might be you next time. We NEVER thought it would be us."

"Keep your faith and live it every day."

"Never, never let your freedoms go."

Even at the age of nine I wanted to be a nurse so I could help others. I received my first degree in nursing at the age of twenty-two. Later, after moving to America, and marrying Ron, I returned to graduate school to get my Masters degree in psychology, and become a licensed, certified psychotherapist. I worked in private practice for many years, specializing in counseling children as well as adults who had PTSD. It seemed as though people who had been severely traumatized gravitated toward me.

Thank you Dad, for being such an amazing person.

LETTERS FROM RUSSIA, 1976-1993

In 1976, fifty-two years after leaving the USSR, Dad finally found the address of his cousins in Bakhmut the family left behind in 1924. He wrote a letter to his cousins, doubting they were still alive and would write back. The following is a copy of the first letter his cousin Maria wrote. Each letter begins or ends with the words, "I wish you wonderful health, both for your body and your soul. I feel so much gratitude for your letter, letting us know you are alive after so many years."

Although their belief in God is never as such mentioned in the letters, they occasionally add, "God bless you." Mostly they write about their health and their relationships with their children and family. The government is never mentioned. At the end of several letters she writes, "We will see you again. If not here, then over there."

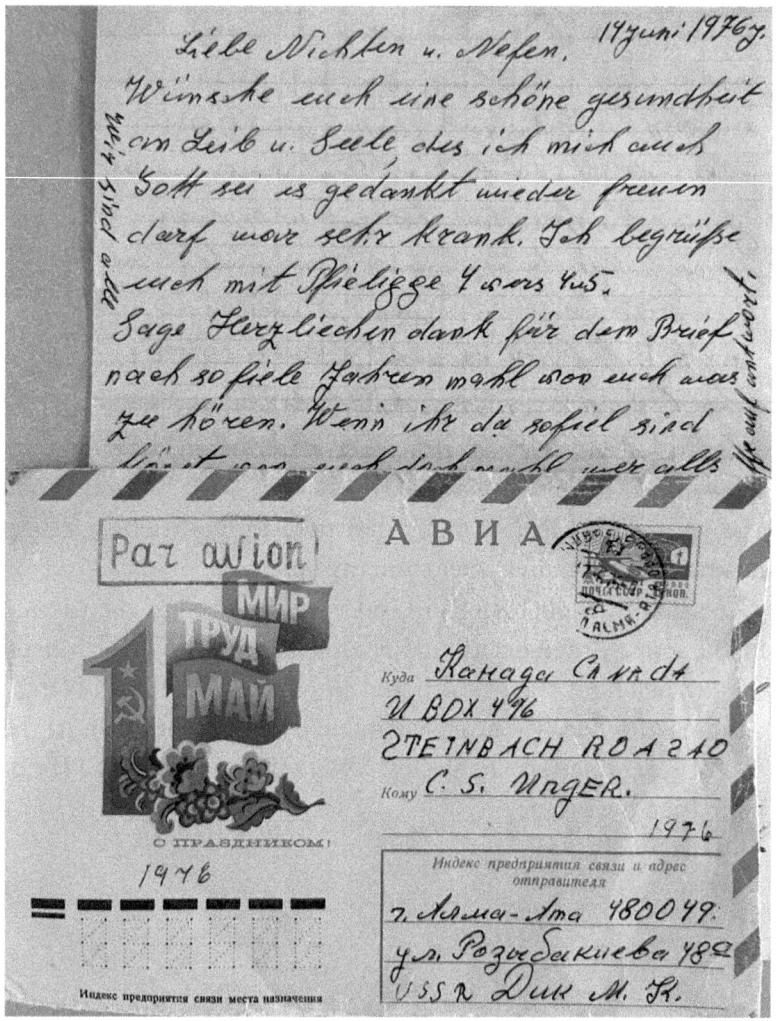

NAME CHANGES IN CANADA

Most of the family members changed their names somewhat when they were registered in Canada, to what they considered to be more acceptable in their new country.

Cornelius—Cornelius—Chnals

Helena—Helen

Sara—Sara

Justina—Jessie

Gerhard—George

Katerina—Teena

Maria—Mary

Anna—Anne

Elizabetha—Betty

ACKNOWLEDGEMENTS

I would like to say thank you to all the people who have encouraged me, read my drafts, and helped me in the writing of this book. I particularly give thanks to my editor Jennifer Leo, the staff at Bitterroot Mountain Publishing House, and my weekly editing group.

www.ingramcontent.com/pod-product-compliance
Lightning Source LLC
Chambersburg PA
CBHW072343100426
42738CB00049B/1600